Beyond
Lewis & Clark

Beyond Lewis & Clark

THE ARMY EXPLORES THE WEST

JAMES P. RONDA

Washington State Historical Society
Tacoma
2003

BEYOND LEWIS & CLARK

The Army Explores the West

EXHIBITION VENUES AND DATES

Virginia Historical Society, Richmond, Virginia: *July 1 through December 30, 2003*
Washington State History Museum, Tacoma, Washington: *February 14 through October 31, 2004*
Kansas History Center, Topeka, Kansas: *December 10, 2004, through August 14, 2005*
Missouri Historical Society, St. Louis, Missouri: *October 8 through December 31, 2005*
Frontier Army Museum, Fort Leavenworth, Kansas: *from April, 2006*

EXHIBITION CREDITS

MANAGING PARTNER: Washington State Historical Society, in association with
Virginia Historical Society, Kansas State Historical Society, and Frontier Army Museum

SPONSORED BY: United States Army Center of Military History, Army Historical Foundation,
The Boeing Company, and Lockheed Martin Aeronautics Company

SPECIAL ACKNOWLEDGMENTS: The Honorable Norm Dicks, Memb er of Congress;
The Honorable John Warner, United States Senator; and Brigadier General John Sloan Brown,
Chief of Military History

PROJECT TEAM: Consulting Historian—James P. Ronda, University of Tulsa; Project Manager—
Redmond J. Barnett, Washington State Historical Society; Managing Curator—John W. Listman, Jr.,
Washington State Historical Society; Coordinator—Stephanie Lile, Washington State Historical
Society; Project Registrar—AnnMarie Price, Virginia Historical Society; Image Acquisition—Lynette
Miller, Washington State Historical Society; Educational Publications—Mary Madden, Kansas State
Historical Society; Contracting Officer—Steven M. Bavisotto, Center of Military History

EXHIBITION DESIGN: Threshold studio

WASHINGTON STATE HISTORICAL SOCIETY
1911 Pacific Avenue
Tacoma, Washington 98402

BOOK DESIGN: Christina Dubois
COVER ART: Threshold studio
Printed in the United States of America by Johnson-Cox Company.

Library of Congress Cataloging-in-Publication Data

Ronda, James P., 1943-
  Beyond Lewis & Clark : the Army explores the West / James P. Ronda.
    p. cm.
Includes bibliographical references.
  ISBN 0-295-98356-6 (pbk.)
  1. West (U.S.)—Discovery and exploration. 2. United States. Army. Corps of Topographical Engineers—History. 3. United States. Army—History—19th century. 4. Explorers—West (U.S.)—History—19th century. 5. Explorers—West (U.S.)—Biography. I. Title: Beyond Lewis and Clark. II. Title.
  F591.R56 2003
  917.804'2—dc21

For Bill Goetzmann

Contents

List of Maps

Acknowledgments

*W*riters write alone but never work alone. Through more than twenty-five years of writing about the exploration of the American West, I have been aided and abetted by a host of colleagues and friends. The list is long; my gratitude is boundless. *Beyond Lewis and Clark* came into being thanks to conversations with David Nicandri, director of the Washington State Historical Society, and Redmond J. Barnett, the society's head of exhibits. They sought—and I hope I have written—a short book that would be a companion piece to an exhibition entitled *Beyond Lewis and Clark: The Army Explores the West*. I remain grateful to Dave and Redmond for the opportunity to be part of so lively and compelling a project. This book marches in company with the exhibition and I am grateful to Threshold studio's Jim Sims and script writer John Styron for their important help along the way.

No one can write about western exploration in general and the role of the United States Army in particular without acknowledging the vast contributions made by William H. Goetzmann. His trilogy—*Army Exploration in the American West, 1803-1863* (1959), *Exploration and Empire: The Explorer and the Scientist in the Winning of the American West* (1966), and *New Lands, New Men: America and the Second Great Age of Discovery* (1986)— both dominates and in large measure defines the field. Like so many others who have written about western exploration, I have been inspired and challenged by Bill Goetzmann's brilliant books. *Beyond Lewis and Clark* is my personal thank-you to him from an admirer on the other side of the Red River.

Closer to home I have found a second home in the Special Collections Department at the University of Tulsa's McFarlin Library. Thanks to the energetic leadership of Lori Curtis, the department now holds a magnificent collection documenting the history of western exploration. I remain grateful to Lori and staff members Milissa Burkart and Gina Minks for their unfailing friendship and constant good cheer. And as always I am deeply indebted to two companions on the trail—my wife Jeanne and my longtime colleague and friend, John L. Allen, who I also thank for his invaluable help in locating important maps.

For what is good here I give thanks to my friends and teachers; for what goes astray I alone am responsible.

—*James P. Ronda*

Thomas Jefferson

Chapter 1

LEWIS AND CLARK—CAPTAINS WEST

The story of the United States Army in the American West is often told in a series of freeze-frames from a Hollywood movie. In quick succession there are images of frontier forts, long columns of mounted troopers, desperate encounters with Indians, all culminating in the obligatory scene of George Armstrong Custer's Seventh Cavalry at the Little Big Horn. For all their importance as cultural icons, these powerful pictures obscure a different and perhaps more important story. For nearly a century—from 1803 until the late 1870s—the army led the way in exploring the West. Soldier-explorers—many of them members of the elite Corps of Topographical Engineers—marched into the West, mapping mountains and rivers, collecting plants and animals, and describing native inhabitants and cultures. Their published reports, maps, drawings, and photographs amounted to a grand encyclopedia of the West. What began with Thomas Jefferson and the Corps of Discovery expedition led by Meriwether Lewis and William Clark became one of the army's most important and influential missions. No story of the American West is complete without recounting the travels of soldier-explorers like Zebulon Montgomery Pike, Stephen H. Long, John Charles Frémont, William H. Emory, and George M. Wheeler. These are names mostly lost to us now. At best we remember Pike for a piece of Colorado mountain geography. And Frémont—once the nation's beloved "Pathfinder"—is now a dim memory from some nearly forgotten history course. But the journeys of the soldier-explorers shaped the course of America's western empire. Following the traces of their journeys, we track the American journey.

Thomas Jefferson was neither a soldier nor an explorer, but as president and commander-in-chief he sent the army into the West with a compelling exploration mission. Like his contemporaries, Jefferson believed that exploration began with journeys into the country of the mind. Behind every expedition was a whole cluster of ideas, plans, ambitions, and illusions. For Jefferson those ideas and mental excursions were all wrapped up in reading. While he was a voracious reader and once told John Adams, "I cannot live without books," opportunities for reading were often hard to come by in a busy presidency.[1] But

William Clark

one of those came each summer when Jefferson fled Washington's oppressive humidity and political heat for Monticello's mountain coolness. In the summer of 1802 Jefferson spent time reading and studying two new acquisitions—the most recent Aaron Arrowsmith "Map of North America" and the just-published *Voyages from Montreal* by Alexander Mackenzie. *Voyages from Montreal* detailed Mackenzie's searches for an overland water route from Atlantic to Pacific, including his epic journey to the Pacific in 1793. While most of Mackenzie's book recounted his travels, the last pages of the final chapter shocked Jefferson into action. In just a few paragraphs Mackenzie sketched out the dimensions of a new British Empire in North America, a grand domain that swept from ocean to ocean. One sentence summed up Mackenzie's bold Columbia River imperial strategy. "By opening this intercourse between the Atlantic and Pacific Oceans, and forming regular establishments through the interior, and at both extremes, as well as along the coasts and islands, the entire command of the fur trade of North America might be obtained."[2] But Mackenzie envisioned more than a fur trade empire. Centering his attention on the world of the Columbia, he urged Great Britain to occupy the West, making it a land of homes and farms.

Few things could anger the president more than the possibility of a British occupation of the West. Mackenzie's proposal touched Jefferson's deep-seated anti-British sentiments at the very time when tensions with Spain and France were mounting. But most important was Jefferson's own vision of the West in the future of the young republic. By the summer of 1802 the president was convinced that the nation's continued political and cultural vitality depended on agricultural settlement in the West. Like many other eighteenth-century social theorists, he believed that the republican virtues of independence, self-reliance, and civic responsibility thrived best in rural, agricultural settings. Those virtues—and American independence itself—would be in danger should Americans slide into urban, industrial ways. If the British lion seized the West before the American eagle came to nest there, the entire experiment in republican government might ultimately fail. The West was, so Jefferson thought, the nation's insurance policy. The Lewis and Clark expedition and the march of the soldier-explorers began the moment Jefferson read Mackenzie.

This was not the first time Jefferson had cast himself as an exploration patron. In 1783, after hearing rumors about Canadian traders heading into the Far West, he asked Revolutionary War hero George Rogers Clark to consider leading an American expedition to thwart British ambitions. Clark, already disabled and deep in debt, declined. As historian Donald Jackson writes, this "was hardly a plan; it was merely a suggestion."[3] Three years later, when he was American ambassador in Paris, Jefferson encountered the star-crossed adventurer John Ledyard. Ledyard's self-styled "passage to glory" began when he served as a corporal of marines on board one of the vessels in Captain James Cook's third Pacific voyage. On that journey Ledyard

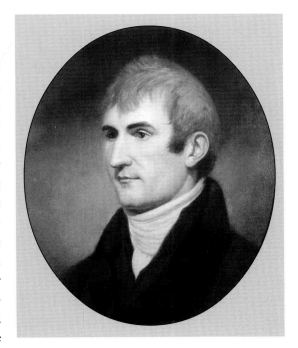

Meriwether Lewis

became fascinated with the possibilities of the China trade and routes across the American continent. Jefferson provided funds for Ledyard's ill-conceived walk across Siberia and later thought the adventurer might hike the American continent from east to west.

But it was not until 1793—the very year that Mackenzie made his continental crossing—that Jefferson had his first real opportunity to plan a western expedition. When André Michaux—botanist and sometime French secret agent—approached the American Philosophical Society with a plan to cross the continent by way of the Missouri and Columbia Rivers, Jefferson was quickly enthusiastic. His reading in exploration and travel literature convinced him that a successful expedition required a comprehensive set of instructions. In many ways the document he drafted for Michaux was the rough draft of what was prepared a decade later for Lewis. Michaux did not get beyond Kentucky, but the whole venture became part of Jefferson's education as an exploration planner.

Wide reading and personal experience joined hands by the end of 1802 as Jefferson made plans for an American response to Mackenzie and the British challenge. In the long history of Euro-American exploration there were many kinds of expeditions, each with its own set of motives and organizational schemes. Missionaries like the Jesuits made hazardous excursions deep into Indian country, hoping to save souls for the Kingdom of God. Merchants and traders, often representing firms like the Hudson's Bay Company or the North West Company, worked their way into the American interior in a search for fur and markets. Adventurers straight out of medieval romance made epic quests for cities of gold and lost tribes in the land of El Dorado. Land company surveyors looked west and mapped out farms and towns in the Ohio country. And there were the soldiers like young George Washington who explored and described what are now West Virginia and western Pennsylvania. Experience with George Rogers Clark, John Ledyard, and André Michaux made it clear to Jefferson that solitary adventurers stood little chance of accomplishing complex exploration missions. Jefferson had to decide what model to use as he planned his response to Mackenzie. Would he hire civilian traders based in St. Louis? Could employees from the federally operated fur trading posts lead such a journey? Might his scholarly friends in Philadelphia be willing to venture across the continent?

Faced with this crucial organizational decision, Jefferson fell back on his reading. And the lessons from that reading were plain. The most successful, large-scale expeditions were organized along military lines. This was the age of Captain James Cook and Captain George Vancouver, a time when Great Britain used its navy to map a world empire. And in that enterprise no one was more influential than Sir Joseph Banks. Longtime president of the Royal Society, de facto director of the royal botanical garden at Kew, and informal scientific advisor to the government of George III, Banks was England's foremost exploration patron. For Banks, voyages of scientific discovery were always in the service of empire. And no private or company expedition could possibly marshal the resources necessary to create what British politician Edmund Burke called "the great map of mankind." While historians often point to the personal relationship between President Jefferson and his private secretary, Captain Meriwether Lewis, as the origin of the American military exploration tradition, we should not overlook the scope of Jefferson's reading and thinking. Jefferson read the English exploration accounts, knew about Banks, and made a clear policy decision. The first American exploring party sent into the West would be a military venture. What Banks and the Royal Navy had done for Great Britain, Jefferson and the United States Army would now attempt for the American republic.

Attorney General Levi Lincoln once told Jefferson that what became the Lewis and Clark expedition was an enterprise of "national consequence."[4] Like Secretary of the Treasury Albert Gallatin—Jefferson's other trusted exploration advisor—Lincoln understood the importance of placing western exploration in army hands. But it would take more than energetic officers and hard-working enlisted men to succeed at what Jefferson began to call "Mr. Lewis's tour." British explorers always set sail with comprehensive instructions, a kind of program based on Enlightenment ideas about direct observation, detailed record-keeping, and careful classification of plant and animal specimens. Jefferson had made an early attempt at preparing such directions for André Michaux. Now Lewis's journey demanded a far more expansive set of marching orders.

Thomas Jefferson believed that human history could be shaped by the power of the written word. The Declaration of Independence, the draft Constitution for the State of Virginia, the Bill for Establishing Religious Freedom, and the Report on Government for Western Territory are all examples of his effort to use words to change history. The exploration instructions prepared for Lewis in June 1803 fit that category. The document was more than just orders from one visionary president to a dutiful young officer. The instructions became the charter for virtually all federal exploration in the nineteenth-century West. Because the letter played so central a role in the army's exploration mission, we should pay special attention to what Jefferson wrote for Lewis. The president drafted a remarkably flexible exploration plan, one that had a single core mission with many secondary objectives. Jefferson summed up that central mission in one sentence: "...to explore the Missouri river, & such principal stream of it, as, by it's course and communication with the waters of the Pacific ocean, whether the Columbia, Oregon, Colorado or any other river may offer the most direct and practicable water communication across the

Sir Joseph Banks

continent for the purposes of commerce."[5] This was the elusive Northwest Passage, Jefferson's version of a dream that had tantalized explorers and their patrons since the age of Columbus. Jefferson sent his soldier-explorers in search of a water highway; in the following decades other soldier-explorers would march west looking for highways suited to the needs of wagons and iron horses. For Jefferson it was not only a route to the riches of India and China but a passage into the fertile lands of the West. This was, as historical geographer John L. Allen has written, "a passage through the garden."[6] Once the passage was found it would be the highway linking American farmers to world markets.

But the president did not intend to march his explorers into the West wearing blinders. Theirs was to be a wide-ranging journey of inquiry. Like his Enlightenment contemporaries, Jefferson believed that truth came from experience as well as research in libraries and laboratories. Explorers made truth by asking questions. While other kinds of expeditions pursued single goals, the Enlightenment approach championed by Banks and the Royal Navy emphasized a broad study of the physical environment and human cultures. Having put the Northwest Passage at the center of the expedition, Jefferson devoted most of the instruction draft to a host of secondary but vital missions.

Ever the literary stylist, the president composed a series of graceful phrases that served to identify and characterize these objectives. The explorers were to describe and map "the face of the country." Expedition journals were soon filled with the most remarkable images of western landscapes as men with East Coast sensibilities struggled to make sense of western realities. Jefferson's travelers were also diplomats and ethnographers, recording "the names of the nations" and acknowledging what William Clark wrote about the expedition's "road across the continent" leading through "a multitude of Indians."[7] Jefferson's instructions contained more questions about native peoples and cultures than any other single topic. After the Louisiana Purchase, Jefferson expanded the expedition's Indian missions to make diplomacy and the presence of a new "Great Father" much more important. And there was the catchall phrase, "other objects worthy of notice"—those objects ranged from astronomy and botany to mineralogy and zoology. All of this was to be written down— "your observations are to be taken with great pains and accuracy"—since knowledge unrecorded could not be shared with a wider world.[8] In retrospect, Jefferson's phrases might be seen as titles for individual volumes in the library of the American West. In future years other soldier-explorers would fill in the outlines and flesh out the chapters.

By the time Jefferson prepared the final draft of instructions for Lewis in June 1803, it was increasingly clear that a successful journey of the sort the president envisioned required more than one officer and a handful of soldiers. Even though the instructions still spoke about a single commander and ten or twelve men, Lewis and Jefferson had already agreed on the necessity of a co-commander and more troops to accomplish so ambitious an exploration program. On June 19, the day before the instructions were formally issued, Lewis wrote William Clark, inviting him to join the journey. What had once looked like a squad heading up the Missouri was rapidly becoming an infantry company on the move.

The recruiting and training of what became the Lewis and Clark expedition is a familiar story. What we call "the Corps of Discovery" was drawn from men of many different racial, ethnic, and occupational backgrounds. Some were soldiers from frontier companies, and not always the best men from those outfits, as William Clark soon learned. Others were hunters with useful skills but unaccustomed to the demands of military order and discipline. And there were French boatmen who possessed valuable river knowledge but resented taking orders from any but their own leaders. One was York, Clark's slave and a man who struggled with his master for freedom in the years after the expedition. Once Sacagawea and her infant son were added to this company, the Corps of Discovery became as diverse as any American community. But making it an effective military community was no easy task.

The winter (1803-04) at Camp Wood outside St. Louis was the expedition's basic training, a time of frequent insubordination, tough talk, and at least one near-mutiny. The first months pushing up the Missouri provided the expedition's shakedown cruise— weeks filled with unpleasant episodes of grumbling, rule-breaking, desertion, and harsh discipline. But by the time the expedition reached the Mandan and Hidatsa earth lodge villages in present-day North Dakota, the captains and their senior sergeant, John Ordway, had succeeded in creating an orderly military community, one founded on army discipline and custom and bound together by a shared sense of mission. Uniforms, flags, detachment orders, inspections, parades, drills, messes, courts-martial, and company punishment—all these marked the expedition as part of the military world. What the captains accomplished was something modern soldiers call "unit cohesion." And that unit cohesion would serve Jefferson's travelers well as they headed across the mountains and down the Columbia to the Great Western Sea.

Nothing tested that unit cohesion more than encounters with strange and often unsettling landscapes. Some of those landscapes were human ones as the expedition met, talked, and traded with a wide variety of native peoples and cultures. Others were all about terrain shapes and weather patterns unlike those in eastern North America. With rare exceptions, the encounters with Native Americans were marked by goodwill and even moments of genuine friendship. At least so it was until the expedition reached the Pacific Coast and spent the winter of 1805-06 among the Clatsops and their neighbors. While native peoples living around the mouth of the Columbia River treated the strangers as one more trading party, Jefferson's travelers viewed those living on the coast with increasing suspicion and hostility. Frustrated by the keen bargaining skills of Chinooks and Clatsops, Lewis and Clark were quick to brand nearby Indians as greedy thieves and untrustworthy neighbors. And difficulties in communication—few members of the expedition learned the Chinook trade jargon—made the cultural distance even greater. Along the Columbia and on the coast, unit cohesion—the powerful sense of community and in-group identity—may have worked against a deeper understanding between Jefferson's explorers and native inhabitants. By drawing in on themselves in a strange place, the expedition may have shut out its neighbors.

But it was not only the human landscape that challenged the Lewis and Clark exploration community in the Northwest. The world of the lower Columbia, especially that volatile environment where the river meets the ocean, was like nothing Lewis and Clark had ever experienced. Here wind and rain mixed with ocean currents and river waves to create a swirl of unpredictable weather and hazardous travel. In mid November 1805 the expedition that had survived blistering heat on the upper Missouri and bitter snows on the Lolo Trail was stranded on the rocky north shore of the Columbia in present-day

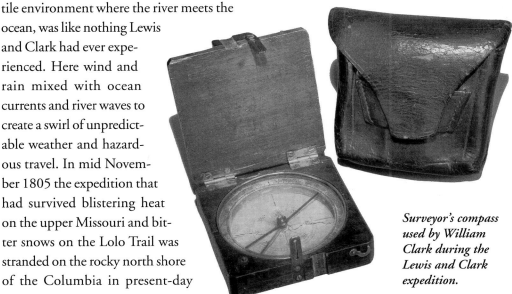

Surveyor's compass used by William Clark during the Lewis and Clark expedition.

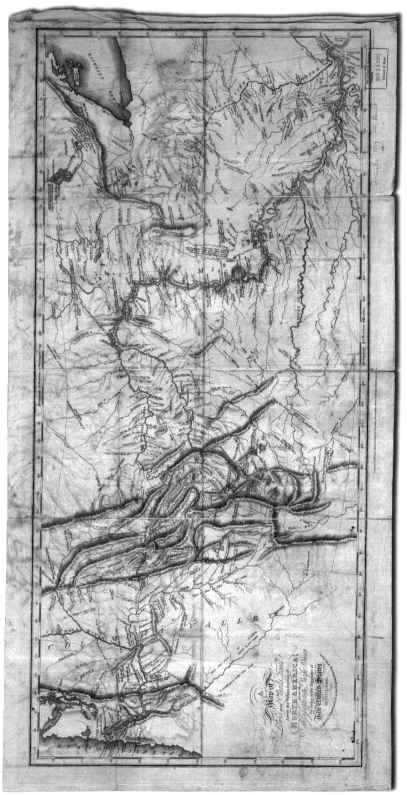

"Map of Lewis and Clark's Track, Across the Western Portion of North America, from the Mississippi to the Pacific Ocean, by Order of the Executive of the United States in 1804, 5 & 6. Copied by Samuel Lewis from the Original Drawing of Wm. Clark."

Washington. What had first seemed an easy sprint to the ocean now bogged down in endless days of rain, high winds, and dangerous river swells. Trapped for nearly a week in a place Clark aptly called "this dismal nitich," getting past present-day Point Ellice seemed almost impossible.[9] Never one to complain, Clark confessed in his journal that these days were "the most disagreeable time I have experienced."[10] And even the quickest look at this infantry company on the move confirmed his assessment. One of the canoes had been shattered on the rocks, food supplies were short, nearby Chinooks seemed wary of the new arrivals, and the explorers' leather clothing was rotting and falling to tatters.

This was a study in frustration. These were the moments that tested the expedition's sense of itself and the ability of Lewis and Clark to make careful decisions and then take appropriate action. With Lewis and a small party already out on a reconnaissance, Clark watched the weather on November 15, waiting for a break in the wind and rain. After a false start early in the morning the weather brightened and the wind slackened later that afternoon. Seizing the opportunity, Clark ordered the canoes loaded for a quick escape from "the dismal nitich." After rounding Point Ellice—what Clark dubbed "Point Distress" or "Blustery Point"—the expedition pulled its canoes up on a "butifull Sand beech." Heading for high ground, Clark established what has come to be called Station Camp. The next day expedition carpenter Patrick Gass noted that "we are now at the end of our voyage, which has been completely accomplished according to the intent of the expedition."[11]

The westbound voyage may have been over, but there was still much to accomplish. The few days (November 15-24) spent at Station Camp were filled with the sorts of duties and routines that had shaped the expedition from the beginning. Station Camp was as much an experience as a place. Once again unit cohesion proved the glue that held the expedition community together in a new environment. Hunting had always been an essential part of that community. The first day at Station Camp, Clark reported that "our hunters and fowlers killd 2 Deer 1 Crane & 2 ducks."[12] York was also out hunting and bagged his share of game. Trading with native peoples, and the personal relationships that grew out of such deals, also quickly emerged at Station Camp, though not without some considerable cultural confusion. Nearby Chinooks had years of experience with white merchants in the maritime fur business. But these Station Camp strangers were different. They came from the wrong direction at the wrong time of year and did not seem to understand the rules of exchange. Even before they were settled in at Fort Clatsop, trade became a source of tension and misunderstanding between the Americans and their native suppliers. But there was one sort of exchange that did go smoothly. On November 21, near the end of the Station Camp sojourn, a Chinook man named Delashelwilt and his wife (a woman Lewis and Clark came to call "the Old Baud") brought six young women to establish a camp near where the Americans had built temporary huts. A thriving, intimate trade soon developed, one that followed the expedition when it moved across the river to Fort Clatsop.

Hunting and trade were the daily affairs that marked out the days at Station Camp. But these soldier-explorers needed to do more than merely keep body and soul together. Just as at other camps, the explorers busied themselves with the kinds of scientific pursuits that Jefferson's instructions detailed. There were plants and animals to describe, Indian objects and foods to comment on, and the terrain itself to evaluate. In several long journal entries Clark took careful note of Chinook clothing, baskets, diet, and physical appearance. But nothing occupied him more than exploring, surveying, and mapping the country around Station Camp and toward the ocean. His survey of the Station Camp landscape is a model for the kind of topographic work that Clark did so well. Beginning on November 18 Clark and eleven men undertook an important reconnaissance from Station Camp to the coast. What the explorers did at Station Camp was a microcosm for its life on the way West. Those few days at camp on the Columbia point us to what future soldier-explorers would do as they marched the West and charted the outlines of an emerging American empire.

The Lewis and Clark expedition stands at the beginning of the American exploration of the West. The details of this emblematic journey are so fascinating, it is easy to forget that the expedition was a military company marching on orders from the commander-in-chief and advancing what became the American empire. In 1802-03 Thomas Jefferson made two fundamental decisions with far-reaching consequences. First, he made exploring the West a federal priority. This was not merely a matter of presidential dreams and congressional funds. Jefferson gave the army its exploration mission. That decision was based on expediency—there was no other national institution capable of completing such a mission—and a wide knowledge of European exploration strategies. Second, and equally important, the president did not imagine his soldier-explorers as mere scouts reconnoitering the positions held by rival European powers or potentially hostile native nations. Instead, he envisioned them as thoughtful observers and collectors engaged in a series of extensive surveys, all designed to produce many kinds of useful knowledge. Writing in 1805, Jefferson confidently predicted that future American explorers would be like artists "fill[ing] up the canvas we begin."[13] In the years after Lewis and Clark, soldier-explorers would go a long way toward "filling up" the western canvas.

Chapter

THE ADVENTURES OF
ZEBULON MONTGOMERY PIKE

History has not been kind to Zebulon Montgomery Pike. Described by one scholar as "the poor man's Lewis and Clark," Pike is now remembered for a Colorado mountain he neither named nor climbed.[1] Cursed by large ambition, an inadequate education, and loyalty to an undeserving commanding officer, Pike struggled to be part of Jefferson's enlarged Corps of Discovery. Despite his best efforts, Pike could never escape the shadow of General James Wilkinson, one of the early West's most dangerous men.

Any story about Pike must begin with Wilkinson. Born in Maryland in 1757, Wilkinson seemed destined for a medical and scientific career when he attended the University of Pennsylvania. Though he did have a genuine interest in natural history, Wilkinson's ambitions always ran more toward wealth and power than to the life of the mind. Marriage to Ann Biddle of the prominent Philadelphia Biddle family only whetted his appetite for the trappings of privilege and the good life. His service in the American Revolution as Clothier-General was not especially distinguished; he succeeded in antagonizing everyone, including George Washington.

After the Revolution, Wilkinson went to Kentucky and soon became part of several ill-conceived conspiracies to separate that territory from the new nation. It was in Kentucky that Wilkinson became a Spanish secret agent, a decision that had little to do with ideology and everything to do with financial gain. In the early 1790s Wilkinson returned to the army as an officer in General Anthony Wayne's Ohio country command. Wayne's unexpected death in late 1796 suddenly opened the way for Wilkinson to become commanding general of American forces on the frontier. Known to his Spanish handlers as "Agent Thirteen," Wilkinson added the governorship of Upper Louisiana to his repertory in 1805. He had already betrayed Lewis and Clark, urging the Spanish to send troops to stop the American explorers. Now a complex set of personal ambitions and international tensions made Wilkinson an exploration planner and patron.

Zebulon Montgomery Pike

Throughout 1804 Wilkinson bombarded Secretary of War Henry Dearborn with reports detailing Spanish military activity along the poorly defined Louisiana Purchase border. In early February 1805 Dearborn finally authorized a secret reconnaissance into present-day Texas. That summer Wilkinson went in search of someone to lead that mission. By the time he visited Fort Massac in present-day Illinois, Wilkinson had not one expedition but two in mind. There was to be a foray into Texas and a scouting mission up the Mississippi River. At Fort Massac Wilkinson met Pike, then district paymaster for the First Infantry Regiment. What drew Wilkinson to Pike remains unclear. The general did know Colonel Zebulon Pike, young Pike's father; Pike's wife Clarissa was the daughter of a Kentucky friend. For whatever reasons, the ambitious Pike was now lured into Wilkinson's world, a place of shadow and intrigue.

Pike's first mission was a "tour of discovery" up the Mississippi. Exploration instructions Wilkinson drafted for Pike in late July 1805 sound much like those Jefferson composed for Lewis—but Pike was Wilkinson's man, not Jefferson's. The Pike expedition was directed to chart the river, observe the region's natural resources, make note of places for commercial and military establishments, and organize Indian delegations for meetings in St. Louis. Always looking to do more, Pike virtually rewrote his orders, giving himself two additional tasks: finding the headwaters of the Mississippi and launching a diplomatic offensive against Canadian traders doing business in present-day Minnesota. By the end of April 1806 Pike and the men he called his "Dam'd set of Rascels" were back in St. Louis. While the soldier-explorer was proud of his maps and observations, Wilkinson muttered that Pike had "stretched his orders."[2]

In his own mind Pike probably believed that the journey up the Mississippi now made him an explorer equal to Lewis and Clark. What the young lieutenant did not know was that his future as a western traveler now rested in the hands of other men with more sinister ambitions. Wilkinson was already in league with Aaron Burr, former vice-president and man on the run after his fatal duel with Alexander Hamilton. While scholars continue to debate the exact nature of the scheme, it is plain that Wilkinson and Burr had set their sights on the West. Whatever their plans—whether invading Mexico, or establishing a new republic in the Southwest, or both—there was increased pressure on Wilkinson to launch a reconnaissance into the lands claimed by Spain.

No more than a month and a half after returning from his Mississippi adventure, Pike found himself assigned to a mission he believed would be "long and Ardious."[3] Formal instructions written by Wilkinson laid out three objectives: the return of Osage prisoners taken captive by the Potawatomis, now ransomed as a sign of American good faith; peace negotiations between Kansas and Osage Indians; and finally, a meeting with the Comanches to establish an anti-Spanish alliance on the central plains. While Pike and Wilkinson insisted that the first two objectives were the expedition's primary missions, it is plain that neither the general nor the lieutenant believed that. It was the third mission—finding the Comanches—that occupied most of Pike's exploration energies and proved most explosive.

Both Wilkinson and Pike knew that any search for the Comanches would inevitably lead Americans into Spanish territory. Wilkinson said as much when he wrote that Pike's journey would take him "approximate to the settlements of New Mexico." Recognizing that Pike would surely enter Spain's Internal Provinces, Wilkinson urged his explorer to "move with great circumspection."[4] Pike was on a spying mission. What remains uncertain is the extent of that mission and who was to benefit from it. How much of this Pike either knew or understood is now lost to us. In a letter he wrote to Wilkinson just days after leaving St. Louis, Pike declared that a journey to Santa Fe under Spanish guard "would gratify our most sanguine expectations."[5] But the nature of those expectations was something neither Pike nor Wilkinson ever committed to paper.

Exploration is all about expectations and the collision of those expectations with the hard realities of weather, landscape, and the unpredictable actions of human beings. Pike's mission—and the route decisions he made along the way—was built on an enticing geographic illusion. Wilkinson, Jefferson, Pike, and nearly everyone else who gave systematic thought to western geography were convinced that the sources of the Red and Arkansas rivers were close together. According to widely accepted lore, the Red rose just east of Taos. This vision of southwestern rivers seemed confirmed by Alexander von Humboldt's "General Map of the Kingdom of New Spain"—a map that Pike knew about and had evidently consulted. With a conjectural geography so at odds with reality, it is little wonder that Pike soon became confused and then terribly lost.

By mid October 1806 Pike's expedition, now numbering some twenty men and including Wilkinson's son James, was at the Great Bend of the Arkansas River. Dividing his expedition into two parties, Pike sent a small detachment commanded by young Wilkinson back down the river to St. Louis. Pike thought he could lead the main body along the Arkansas and then easily scout the Red. And somewhere along the way he would meet the Comanches as well. Early December 1806 found Pike's men—still wearing summer uniforms as they had neglected to take winter clothing along—just below present-day Canon City, Colorado, where the Arkansas comes through the Royal Gorge. A brief reconnaissance revealed two creeks, the Grape and the Oil. Pike now made the first of several fateful choices. Believing that he had found the headwaters of the Arkansas and confident that the Red was nearby, he decided to follow what he thought was a fresh Spanish trail heading north. Pike then planned to swing south toward Santa Fe and the waters of the Red River. Considering Pike's image of western geography, such a plan was neither illogical nor foolhardy. It turned out to be both.

As the plan unfolded, Pike's expedition traveled north to the South Platte River and then turned west to intercept the main stem of the Arkansas—a stream Pike was sure was the Red. By mid December 1806 Pike and his men were in deep trouble. Still clad in light uniforms, they now faced a Rockies winter and an uncertain future. Pike admitted that he was lost. "The geography of the country had turned out to be so different from our expectations; we were at some loss which course to pursue."[6] It was not until January 1807 that Pike finally realized that the Arkansas was not the Red.

Having made one wrong choice, Pike now made another. Hampered by inadequate supplies and lacking horses, Pike confessed that "I now felt at a considerable loss how to proceed."[7] If he turned down the Arkansas and then marched south, he would strike the north fork of the Canadian River. If the expedition traveled southwest and crossed the Sangre de Cristo Mountains the explorers would come upon the Rio Grande. No matter what, Pike was sure to believe he had at last found the elusive Red. On January 9 Pike made his choice and for eighteen terrible days he and his men struggled through the snows of the Sangre de Cristo and finally reached the San Luis Valley in present-day south central Colorado. Up the Conejos River and near present-day Alamosa, Pike's men built a log stockade and hoisted the American flag. Sure he was finally on the Red, Pike was equally confident he was still within the boundaries of the Louisiana Purchase. But in 1807 all the West was suspect terrain and few things were more uncertain than the boundaries of the purchase.

Pike's confidence was shaken on the morning of February 26, 1807, when two Spanish scouts appeared. These men were the advance detail for a large party led by Lieutenants Ignatio Saltelo and Bartholomew Fernandez. Stunned by news that he was on the Rio Grande and within Spanish territory, Pike exclaimed, "What...is not this the Red river[?]."[8] Pike and his men then went under guard to Santa Fe. Pike's claim that he was lost and had stumbled into Spanish territory has often been doubted as an obvious ruse. Those who argue that Pike deliberately entered New Mexico and hoped to fall into Spanish hands point to the Wilkinson-Dearborn scheme for secret probes into the Southwest and the letter Pike sent to Wilkinson soon after leaving St. Louis. Pike acknowledged that a search for the Comanches might take him outside the boundaries of the United States and should that happen he might claim to be lost. But by the time Spanish forces found him, Pike was lost and hopelessly so.

For the next four months Pike and his unfortunate soldiers traveled under Spanish guard. Their route passed through Santa Fe and then into present-day Mexico. After some time in Chihuahua, the party marched northeast across the Sierra Madre Oriental

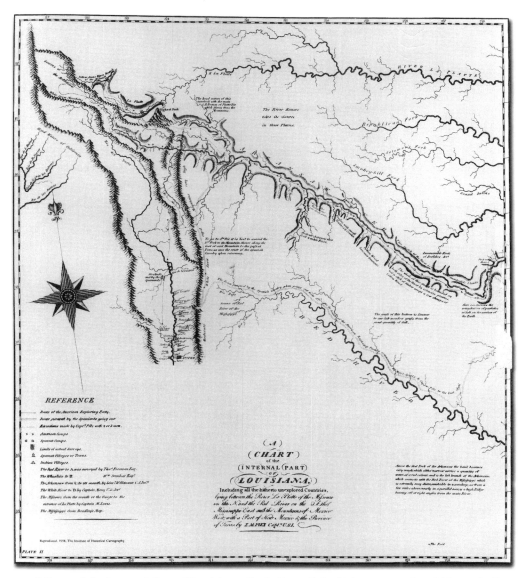

"Chart of the Internal Part of Louisiana, Including all the hitherto unexplored Countries,"
by Zebulon M. Pike, 1810.

Mountains and into present-day Texas. After a brief stay in San Antonio, Pike and his men reached American soil in late June 1807.

Lewis and Clark had already been back from their western tour of duty for almost a year and were enjoying considerable public acclaim. Pike came back as neither a hero nor a successful spy. As Donald Jackson has written, "Nothing that Pike ever tried to do was easy, and much of his luck was bad."[9] And that bad luck continued as Pike sought unsuccessfully to gain recognition and reward for himself and his men. Pike's *Account of Expeditions to the Sources of the Mississippi, and Through the Western Parts of Louisiana* (1810) appeared four years before any official Lewis and Clark report, but the explorer's manuscript was so badly organized that publisher John Conrad wondered in print "whether any book ever went to press under so many disadvantages as the one now presented to the public."[10]

Overshadowed by Lewis and Clark and tainted by association with Wilkinson and Burr, Pike has steadily slipped from grace and national memory. Pike's untimely death in action during the War of 1812 made him a momentary hero but a quickly forgotten explorer. Nonetheless, Pike stands at the beginning of a whole parade of soldier-explorers fascinated with the Southwest. That fascination was not simply with a landscape unlike any familiar to eastern eyes and seemingly exotic cultures. Beginning with Pike, soldier-explorers looked to the Southwest as part of an expanding American empire. Pike said as much in 1808 when he wrote, "Should an army of Americans ever march into the country...they will have only to march from province to province in triumph, and be hailed by the united voices of grateful millions as their deliverers and saviors, whilst our national character would be resounded to the utmost distant nations of the earth."[11] Many of Pike's successors in the Corps of Topographical Engineers would share that dream and that passion.

Chapter

STEPHEN H. LONG—INTO THE PLAINS

By 1812 soldier-explorers and fur traders had extended American influence up the Mississippi and Missouri and into the Yellowstone country. John Jacob Astor's Pacific Fur Company planted itself at Astoria at the mouth of the Columbia River. And at least a few St. Louis merchants, along with Pike, dreamed of a southwestern reach as well. But this first American empire in the West—built largely on the fur business—was swept away in the War of 1812. Textbook accounts of that war often emphasize its Atlantic and East Coast events, with colorful descriptions of the star-spangled banner at Fort McHenry, the burning of Washington, D.C., and the Battle of New Orleans. But the war had profound consequences in the West beyond St. Louis. Northern plains Indians renewed their trade and diplomatic alliances with Canadian traders, driving Americans out of the upper Missouri and upper Mississippi countries. Hearing that war was declared, Astor's Canadian employees at Astoria promptly sold the firm and the post to the North West Company. When British naval forces arrived on the Columbia in December 1813, Astoria was already renamed Fort George and flying the Union Jack. At war's end in 1814 the first American empire in the West was in ruins.

By the time President James Monroe's administration came to Washington in 1817, it was plain that the United States needed to reassert its influence in the lands of the Louisiana Purchase. William Clark, now territorial governor and superintendent of Indian Affairs for the West, had already begun a series of Indian councils that eventually produced a whole series of fence-mending treaties. At the same time, the War Department undertook a review of western defenses that resulted in the construction of posts from Fort Snelling on the upper Mississippi to Fort Smith on the Arkansas River. But no one was more forceful in calling for a renewed American presence on the frontier than Secretary of War John C. Calhoun. Working in conjunction with expansionist-minded Secretary of State John Quincy Adams, Calhoun developed an ambitious plan for the army to show the flag in the trans-Mississippi West. Eventually known in the popular press as the Yellowstone Expedition, Calhoun's scheme actually involved two distinct troop movements: the Mississippi Expedition led by Colonel Henry Leavenworth and the Missouri Expedition under the command of Colonel Henry Atkinson. By 1819 Calhoun and the War Department envisioned moving some one thousand troops up these rivers. Transport would be provided by steamboats, a new technology that Secretary Calhoun believed would be efficient and might at the same time impress native peoples.

Stephen Harriman Long

The flurry of activity surrounding these preparations attracted the attention of Major Stephen H. Long, an army topographical engineer. Born in New Hampshire in 1784 and educated at Dartmouth College, Long demonstrated a wide-ranging set of interests in everything from mathematics to natural history. In 1814 he joined the army and in December was commissioned as a second lieutenant of engineers. Long proved not only a talented engineer but a skillful politician as well. Thanks to his friendship with General Joseph Swift, then chief of engineers for the army, Long was posted to teach mathematics at West Point for a year. After leaving the military academy in 1816 he began a series of assignments throughout the Mississippi Valley and the Old Northwest. It was that experience—and his growing interest in steamboats—that prepared Long to organize and lead what became the army's first scientific reconnaissance of the central Great Plains.

It was steamboats that first brought Long and Calhoun together in June 1818. Long was convinced that he could build a steam-powered craft that might safely navigate shallow western waters. After listening to Long, Calhoun was persuaded and ordered the engineer to begin work on the project. At the same time, Long began to consider a scientific expedition as part of Atkinson's Missouri River venture. He was not the first to make this suggestion; members of the American Philosophical Society had proposed such an expedition some time before. But Long enjoyed Calhoun's confidence and as he built the steamboat in Pittsburgh he also began to assemble a team of civilian scientists who would be the core of his Scientific Expedition.

Thomas Jefferson once complained that western expeditions "are so laborious and hazardous, that men of science, used to the temperature and inactivity of their closet, cannot be induced to undertake them." When Jefferson wrote those lines in 1806 the American scientific community was small, with slender resources and limited personnel. And western journeys did seem daunting. But Jefferson hoped that some day, "when the route shall be once open and known, scientific men will undertake" such journeys.[1] In the decade after the War of 1812 the president's prophecy seemed to come true. The nation's scientific institutions, centered largely in Philadelphia, matured and grew in size. It was to Philadelphia that Long looked as he began to recruit scholars and artists for his western expedition.

The list of Long's recruits reads like a *Who's Who* of American science. Long's zoologist was Thomas Say, a charter member of the Academy of Natural Sciences in Philadelphia and author of widely respected studies in conchology and entomology. The expedition's first botanist, Dr. William Baldwin, had already done extensive fieldwork in Georgia, Florida, and South America. In poor health, Baldwin evidently hoped that a western journey would prove restorative. While Philadelphia merchant Augustus Jessup was not a professional geologist, he was widely read in the field and was also a member of the Academy of Natural Sciences. Long was acutely aware of the need to provide a visual record of his expedition. While the grand oceanic voyages mounted by Great Britain and Spain carried full complements of artists, no American expedition into the West had yet taken along such a specialist. Illustrated travel accounts were increasingly commonplace; both the reading public and serious scholars now expected exploration reports to contain not only text and maps but graphic depictions of landscapes, Native Americans, and plant and animal specimens. The worlds of art and science had not yet drifted apart as they would later in the century. Long again turned to the Philadelphia natural history community, engaging two talented artists. Recently arrived from England, Samuel Seymour was an able landscape painter. His work would provide American audiences with the earliest published views of the western lands. Titian Ramsay Peale, youngest son of painter and museum entrepreneur Charles Willson Peale, became the expedition's second artist. Like his contemporary, Karl Bodmer, the young Peale was able to capture both the detail and essence of a plant or animal in a series of glowing drawings. To round out the expedition's scientific cadre, Long enlisted Major Thomas Biddle as official record keeper and Lieutenant James D. Graham and Cadet William Swift as personal aides.

Jefferson's instructions to Lewis and Clark set the agenda for federal exploration in the West. The imprint of the Lewis and Clark experience was plain when Secretary Calhoun drafted directions for Long's Scientific Expedition. Rivers remained a focus for both exploration and commercial travel. "You will first explore the Missouri and its principal branches, and then, in succession, Red river, Arkansas and Mississippi, above the mouth of the Missouri." Jefferson's vision of exploration as a broad enterprise with national significance continued as Calhoun told Long that "the object of the Expedition, is to acquire as thorough and accurate knowledge as may be practicable of a portion of our country, which is daily becoming more interesting, but which is as yet imperfectly known." Again sounding much like Jefferson, Calhoun directed Long to "enter in your journal, everything interesting in relation to soil, face of the country, water courses and productions, whether animal, vegetable or mineral." Keenly aware of the relationship between army exploration and federal Indian policy, the secretary reminded Long to "conciliate the Indians by kindness and presents, and...ascertain, as far as practicable, the number and character of the various tribes, with the extent of country claimed by each." And in a final nod to Jefferson's original document, Calhoun concluded by reminding Long that "the instructions of Mr. Jefferson to Capt. Lewis, which are printed in his travels, will afford you many valuable suggestions, of which as far as applicable, you will avail yourself."[2]

In early May 1819 Long's Scientific Expedition set out down the Ohio River from Pittsburgh aboard the appropriately christened *Western Engineer.* What Long had built was no ordinary steamboat. Noting that its paddlewheels were properly named "Monroe" and "Calhoun," Titian Peale joked that this arrangement was fitting since these politicians were "the two propelling powers of the expedition."[3] The vessel's most striking feature was an elaborately carved dragon that served as both steam exhaust and figurehead. As one contemporary newspaper account put it, "The bow of this vessel exhibits the form of a huge serpent, black and scaly, rising out of the water from under the boat, his head as high as the deck, darting forward, his mouth open, vomiting smoke, and apparently carrying the boat on his back."[4] Calhoun and Long continued to hope that steamboats on western waters would impress the Indians with the power of the United

Sketch of Topographical Engineers' cantonment and the expedition steamboat, Western Engineer.

But the *Western Engineer* was anything but impressive. The boat might have been able to make thunderous displays of smoke and fire but she proved less-than-reliable transportation. Cursed with a cranky engine and a leaky cabin, the *Western Engineer* did not arrive in St. Louis until early June.

After two weeks in St. Louis the Scientific Expedition was ready to challenge the Missouri. Long's first goal was to establish a base camp for the winter at Council Bluffs, on the western bank of the Missouri some twenty miles upriver from present-day Omaha, Nebraska. But getting to that site proved a difficult task. As every river traveler knew or soon learned, the Missouri current was a powerful force that tested muscle or engine. And just beneath the surface there were snags and sawyers that could rip the bottom out of any boat. The Long expedition not only struggled against the river but also confronted serious personnel troubles. Long and Biddle had rancorous quarrels, and at one point Biddle rashly challenged his commanding officer to a duel. In failing health, Dr. Baldwin left the expedition in mid July and died a month later. Geologist Augustus Jessup began to have second thoughts about western exploring. Despite these difficulties, the Scientific Expedition managed to reach its winter camp in late September.

Naming his post Engineer Cantonment, Long set about establishing a center for future explorations. The larger Atkinson Missouri Expedition made its Council Bluffs camp nearby at Cantonment Missouri. For both soldiers and civilians the winter of 1819-20 was anything but pleasant. Disease and malnutrition haunted Atkinson's troops. On one day alone Surgeon Thomas Gale reported that there were "two hundred and eighty sick principally with scurvy."[5] Two weeks later, in early March 1820, the surgeon counted seven burials and more than three hundred soldiers on sick report. While the Missouri Expedition suffered in the Great Plains cold, Long's "scientifics" did their best to pursue exploration objectives. Seymour, Peale, Say, Jessup, and guide-interpreter John Dougherty took short trips, gathering important scientific and ethnographic information. But Long's explorers did their work without him. Fearing that the troubles of the Missouri Expedition might spill over to destroy his own venture and perhaps worried about possible federal budget cuts, Long decided to make a quick trip to Washington. Politics—domestic and international—had always been part of the exploration enterprise. Long was soon to discover just how large a part.

By the time Long reached the capitol in early 1820, much had changed. There had always been controversy around the grand Calhoun plan, and now critics in Congress managed to cut funding for the Missouri Expedition. Perhaps those cuts would also extend to the Scientific Expedition, or so Long might have suspected. Even though the Long expedition had accomplished few of its objectives in 1819, Calhoun decided to give the soldier-explorer modest additional funds as well as authorization to engage extra personnel. More important, the Scientific Expedition got new instructions from the War Department. Disputes between the United States and Spain over the southern boundary of the Louisiana Purchase had come to some resolution in the Adams-Onís Treaty of 1819. That treaty proposed the boundary between Louisiana and Spanish territory based on the courses of the Arkansas and Red, rivers that had proved elusive for more than one exploring party. Calhoun now decided that the Scientific Expedition should follow the Platte to its source and then head south to map the Red and the Arkansas.

With orders that sent his expedition on the first American scientific exploration of the central Great Plains now in hand, Long moved to find replacements for Biddle, Baldwin, and Jessup. Biddle's replacement was Captain John R. Bell, a no-nonsense officer eager to escape the routine of garrison life. The most important addition came in the person of Dr. Edwin James. A New Englander like Long, James had studied at Middlebury College in Vermont before joining his brother's medical practice in Albany, New York. But James was no ordinary doctor. He had read widely in a number of scientific fields and had the kind of inquisitive mind essential for western exploration. By late May 1820 Long and his fellow explorers were back at Engineer Cantonment on the Missouri, ready to venture west.

For all his practical engineering abilities, Long proved a remarkably inept expedition planner. There were hints of this in his early, wildly impractical steamboat schemes and in later grandiose exploration schemes submitted to Secretary Calhoun. While Lewis and Clark paid careful attention to matters of equipment and supply, Long let those crucial matters slip. A meager budget did not help, but Long and his men headed west with a food supply good for only one month's travel and a mere six extra horses. Not only was the expedition's supply of trade goods inadequate but boxes necessary to store scientific specimens were in short supply. This was a scientific expedition that seemed unworthy of its formal name.

Despite these obvious shortcomings, the Long expedition—scientists and soldiers alike—rode out of camp in early June heading west. After a short but important visit to the Grand Pawnee village, the explorers reached the Platte River. Near the end of June, Long's party came to the junction of the North and South Platte at present-day North Platte, Nebraska. There they forded the north branch and crossed to the south side of the South Platte. While Long scouted for the river's source, his scientists took note of the Great Plains environment. At a time when Jefferson's vision of the West as the Garden of the World was still geographic gospel, expedition journals began to be filled with words like "barren," "sterile," and "arid." For New Englanders like Long and James the plains landscape was both strange and unsettling. As James wrote later: "The monotony of a vast unbroken plain, like that in which we had now traveled, nearly one hundred and fifty miles, is little less tiresome to the eye, and fatiguing to the spirit, than the dreary solitude of the ocean."[6] In early July the expedition reached present-day Denver and from Pike's Peak the explorers could see the Platte coming from what they took to be its mountain source. Without actually locating and mapping the headwaters, Long claimed that one of Calhoun's objectives had been accomplished.

Thinking he had solved the Platte puzzle, Long led the party south to find the Arkansas. In mid July James and Bell undertook a short reconnaissance around the Royal Gorge

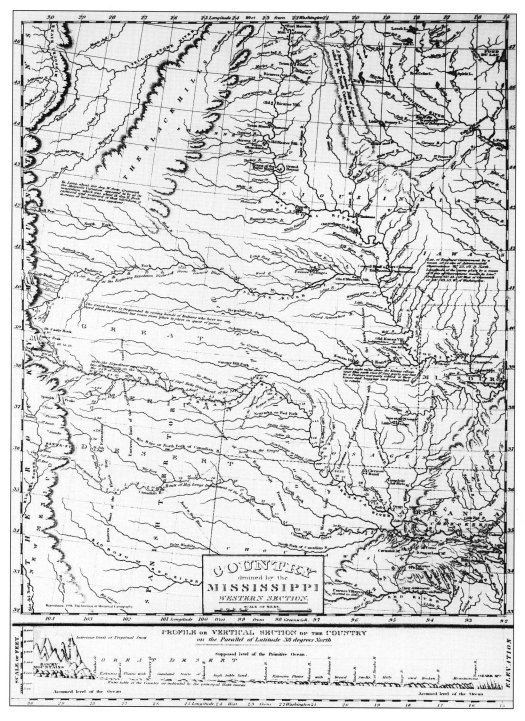

*Map of the "Country drained by the Mississippi, Western Section,"
by Stephen Long, 1823.*

of the Arkansas. Just as he had given the Platte a once-over-lightly treatment, Long decided that he now knew enough about the Arkansas as well. While expedition scientists and artists continued to do their work under difficult conditions, Long laid plans for a homeward journey. Those plans involved dividing the expedition into two traveling parties. Captain Bell was directed to take a small detachment down the Arkansas to Belle Pointe at present-day Fort Smith, Arkansas. Meanwhile, Long's main group would march south to strike the Red and then proceed to join Bell at Belle Pointe. Bell's passage on the Arkansas was anything but smooth. Three of his men deserted, taking with them not only horses and supplies but the field notes complied by Say and Swift. In terms of their mission, Long and his companions suffered the greatest disappointment. Encountering a river they assumed was the Red, they tracked it southeast. Like others before, Long was tricked by the ever-elusive Red. The river Long found was the Canadian, a discovery that in James's words "defeated one principal aspect of our summer's labor."[7] It was not until mid September 1820 that the entire expedition was reunited at Belle Pointe.

It would be easy to dismiss Stephen H. Long as an unworthy successor to the tradition of army exploration established by Jefferson and Lewis and Clark. Long paid scant attention to the necessary details of planning and supply. He was an indecisive field commander who all too often neglected important exploration objectives. More than anything else, Long has been charged as the creator of the "Great American Desert" idea. That phrase was indeed a feature of his important 1823 map. And in his official report to Calhoun, Long declared that large sections of the great plains were "almost wholly unfit for cultivation, and of course uninhabitable by a people depending on agriculture for their subsistence."[8] Like some of his contemporaries, Long also thought that the arid West might serve as a barrier to over-rapid territorial expansion. Such a barrier would also "secure us against the machinations or incursions of an enemy, that might otherwise be disposed to annoy us in that quarter."[9]

Long might have labeled significant portions of the West as desert, but that was never a widespread belief among American settlers, government policy makers, and real estate promoters. For them the West would always be Jefferson's garden. In later years, as farmers on the Great Plains struggled with drought and dust, Long's concerns seemed almost prophetic. Too much emphasis on the Great American Desert idea and Long's failures in the field has tended to diminish the genuine accomplishments of the Scientific Expedition. Long was the first American soldier-explorer to take professional scientists and artists into the West. Paintings and sketches by Seymour and Peale gave visual definition to a West so far set down only in print. Edwin James, author of *Account of an Expedition from Pittsburgh to the Rocky Mountains* (1823), proved an astute observer of western geology and climate. Long's two western maps (1821, 1823) made significant contributions to North American cartography. But, as historians Roger L. Nichols and Maxine Benson have noted, the important scientific contributions of the Long expedition were not recorded in the pages of James's travel narrative. Say, Peale, James, Jessup, and Long all published their findings in a number of scientific journals. The expedition also had an impact on the emerging body of American literature. James Fenimore Cooper used James's *Account* as a sourcebook for his popular novel, *The Prairie* (1827).

Chapter 4

MAKING PROFESSIONAL EXPLORERS

By the end of the 1820s soldier-explorers were becoming an established feature of American exploration in the West. What Jefferson had set in motion was now something of a tradition. But much had changed since the days of Lewis and Clark. While the word "scientist" was not yet part of the American vocabulary, the pursuit of useful knowledge grew more specialized and increasingly the domain of professionals. The day of the amateur naturalist on a tour of the West was rapidly giving way to the age of the highly trained botanist and zoologist. Beginning with the Long expedition, Jefferson's prophecy that scholars would leave their libraries and laboratories seemed to come true. Exploration science, always rooted in the search for useful knowledge, demanded better organization as well as explorers able to satisfy the requirements of an increasingly sophisticated intellectual community.

As part of that larger community the army's soldier-explorers drew strength from two key institutions. The first of those was the United States Military Academy at West Point. Founded by Thomas Jefferson in 1802, the academy became the training ground for two generations of army explorers. In his remarks at the opening of the academy on July 4, 1802, Superintendent Major Jonathan Williams made plain West Point's intellectual ambitions. "Our guiding star," he declared, "is not a little mathematical establishment. We must always have it in view that our officers are to be men of Science, and as such will by their acquirements be entitled to the notice of learned societies."[1] The emerging curriculum at West Point—centering on mathematics, geometry, topographical sketching, and surveying—gave young officers unique preparation to become explorers. Graduates left the academy with a keen eye for geography and topographic detail, and the necessary skills to both describe and evaluate the landscape of a growing nation. Nearly all the officers in the army's Corps of Topographical Engineers were West Point graduates. And in an ironic twist, the most famous of those topographical engineers was not.

If West Point was the training ground for soldier-explorers, then the Corps of Topographical Engineers provided an institutional home. Topographical engineers had been part of the American military establishment since the Revolution. But it was not until the War of 1812 that the army first established a separate topographical engineers unit. At the conclusion of the war in 1814 all but two of the topographical engineers—Isaac Roberdeau and John Anderson—were honorably discharged back into civilian life. When George Washington named Robert Erskine as the Continental Army's first topographical engineer, Erskine was ordered "to take sketches of the country and the seat of war."[2] That order implied missions both in times of war and peace. In the period after the War of 1812 army engineers found themselves posted to all sorts of duties, from surveying sites for future forts and coastal defense locations to internal improvements like roads and canals. Stephen H. Long's early assignments at places like Fort Smith and Fort Snelling were typical of the duties carried out by the engineers. By the early 1820s there was so great a demand for trained civil engineers that Major Roberdeau, then acting chief of the Topographical Bureau, feared that the army could not retain its best West Point graduates. In an annual report to the secretary of war, Roberdeau explained that "no other country in the world feels the want of professional characters [engineers] of this kind as does the United States; nor is there a nation in the world whose prosperity and improvement so much depends upon the establishment of some system by which this deficiency may be supplied."[3]

Major Roberdeau surely understood the challenge but had neither the expansive vision nor the political connections to make the necessary changes. That duty fell to John James Abert. Abert became chief of the Topographical Bureau in 1829. If Thomas Jefferson gave soldier-explorers their charter, it was Abert who gave them their marching orders. Like Jefferson, Abert was both a visionary and a shrewd politician. With single-minded determination Abert created the Corps of Topographical Engineers, sustained it through several dangerous congressional passages, gave it intellectual substance, and energetic leadership. For virtually its entire life as a separate unit—from 1838 until Abert's retirement in 1861— the Corps of Topographical Engineers had one commanding officer, Colonel John J. Abert.

By the time Abert came to direct the Topographical Bureau in 1829 he was already a man of considerable accomplishment. After graduation from West Point in 1811 Abert pursued a part-time law practice and a nearly full-time program of reading in the sciences. But what plainly captured his imagination was the possibility of a topographical engineers unit separate from the regular Corps of Engineers. In Abert's mind such an outfit would have a broad range of missions, with energies and ambitions to match an expanding nation. Writing in 1835, Abert urged the War Department to station "a brigade of officers on the western frontiers."[4]

As Abert worked to create his own corps, he found a powerful ally in Secretary of War Joel R. Poinsett. A remarkable man with large interests and considerable travel experience, Poinsett had already served as a diplomat in Mexico and was something of an amateur naturalist. Named secretary of war in 1837, Poinsett quickly recognized the need to expand Abert's small bureau. Like Abert, the secretary linked soldier-explorers to national expansion and to an ideology that came to be called Manifest Destiny. In his 1838 report to Congress, Poinsett proposed an enlarged Topographical Bureau, admitting, "We are still lamentably ignorant of the geography and resources of our country."[5] Abert and Poinsett were not only bureaucratic allies—they also shared a common view about the nature of western exploration. That such exploration should put science in the service of empire was plain enough. As Abert wrote to Poinsett, "Valuable and useful knowledge will always find a patron in the United States."[6] Poinsett's report to Congress for 1839, prepared the year after the formal establishment of the Corps of Topographical Engineers, offered a clear statement of what the secretary and the unit's new commanding officer had in mind. After urging Congress to fund "researches over the Rocky Mountains to the shores of the Pacific," Poinsett detailed what became "the Abert Plan" for comprehensive scientific exploration. "It is believed that these explorations, cautiously and slowly conducted, will prove much more useful in their results, both as regards the geography and natural history of that portion of our country, than the great expeditions which have preceded them, and which could not devote the time necessary to acquire the accurate information now sought for."[7]

Colonel John J. Abert

When the army underwent major reorganization in 1838, it was clear that Abert and Poinsett had prevailed. As part of the reorganization plan the Topographical Bureau now became the Corps of Topographical Engineers, distinct from the Corps of Engineers and directly responsible to the secretary of war. While the corps never numbered more than 64 officers in its entire organizational life, it became the nation's principal exploring arm in the West. Topographical engineers, educated at West Point and connected to the latest in European and American scientific thinking, saw themselves as representatives of an expansionist nation as well as the larger empire of the mind. Historian William H. Goetzmann aptly describes them in this fashion: "The Topographical Engineers were sophisticated men of their time who worked closely with the foremost scholars in American and European centers of learning. The army topographer considered himself by schooling and profession as one of a company of savants."[8]

Chapter

5

JOHN CHARLES FRÉMONT—
THE PATHFINDER'S WEST

Colonel Abert imagined the Corps of Topographical Engineers as a group of dedicated, well-trained soldier-explorers doing the business of exploration well away from the glare of publicity. Abert was not averse to favorable press, but the notion of explorer-as-celebrity seemed both foolish and dangerous. As fortune would have it, one topographical engineer captured public attention and came to represent the nation's "course of empire." Born in 1813 to Charles Fremon and Ann Beverly Whiting, John Charles Frémont was the child of parents who never married. Forced by scandal to leave Charleston, South Carolina, the Fremons wandered from place to place, "a family," writes Donald Jackson, "of unstable finances."[1]

Much of John Charles Frémont's adult life was shaped by relationships with powerful patrons, a common enough pattern in nineteenth-century America. In 1826 Frémont entered the Charleston law offices of attorney John W. Mitchell. While it appeared that he might have a future in the legal profession, Frémont read widely in the classics and was increasingly drawn to mathematics. Mitchell encouraged Frémont to continue his education and provided tuition for studies at a local preparatory school. In 1829, thanks to a charity scholarship, Frémont entered the College of Charleston's junior class in the Scientific Department. Suggesting something of a pattern that would come to haunt him later, Frémont paid little attention to details like class attendance. Dismissed from the college by an exasperated faculty, he missed graduation by three months and did not receive his degree until five years later.

In the early 1830s Frémont drifted from job to job, occasionally teaching mathematics at several private schools and doing a bit of land surveying as well. It was in those years that Frémont found his second patron in the person of Joel Poinsett. Already a prominent figure in South Carolina, Poinsett was well on his way to national office. It was through Poinsett's influence that young Frémont won a berth on the USS *Natchez* as a mathematics teacher. And in the years 1833-35, as the vessel sailed South American waters, Frémont got his first glimpse of a wider world. At the end of the cruise Frémont hoped to find a permanent position in the navy. When that did not materialize, Poinsett again stepped in, getting Frémont a place on a railroad survey being conduced by the Topographical Bureau. That experience—combining scientific observation and rigorous outdoor travel—convinced Frémont that he should apply for a commission with the topographical engineers. In December 1837—with Poinsett now secretary of war—Frémont made his application.

Mitchell and Poinsett had been essential for Frémont's progress in the world. But it was Joseph Nicolas Nicollet (1786-1843) who shaped him as an explorer. A brilliant geographer and astronomer, Nicollet left France for the United States in 1832. He believed that geographic exploration demanded a comprehensive set of observations done with the best scientific instruments, including barometers to measure altitude. Nicollet's first explorations in the Mississippi Valley were self-financed, but he soon came to the attention of Secretary Poinsett and Colonel Abert. Nicollet represented exactly what Abert and Poinsett hoped the Corps of Topographical Engineers could accomplish. In 1838 and 1839 the War Department funded two Nicollet expeditions into present-day Minnesota and the Dakotas. Frémont's career as an explorer was set in motion in April 1838 when Abert assigned him as Nicollet's assistant. The few letters that survive from these years show a pattern that became clearer over the years. Nicollet's passion for precise calculation and detailed cartography made an enduring impression on Frémont. Letters to Poinsett reported on those efforts. But the same letters also contained stories of adventure and daring. Nicollet taught Frémont exploration as science; Frémont's reading and his own temperament suggested that exploration could also be romantic and colorful.

Frémont's career took yet another turn in April 1841 when the young lieutenant met Jessie Benton, the sixteen-year-old daughter of Missouri senator Thomas Hart Benton. Their whole whirlwind courtship and secret marriage (October 1841) is the stuff of romance novels. Jessie became Frémont's strongest supporter and writing partner. But the dramatic story of their relationship has often obscured the crucial role Senator Benton and Colonel Abert played in making Frémont a western explorer.

By the early 1840s there were few national voices urging territorial expansion louder than Benton's. After a trip to Monticello in 1824 to visit an aging Jefferson, Benton came to believe that the mantle of western expansion had been passed to him. Benton's western perspective grew over the years. At one point he imagined the United States reaching no farther than the Rockies, but the promise of the Oregon country and the lure of trade with China prompted the senator to embrace a more expansive vision. Overcoming his anger at the clandestine marriage, Benton began to see Frémont as the chosen instrument for national expansion. In Benton, Frémont found yet another patron—one who possessed both power and vision.

Abert, Poinsett, and Nicollet always championed a careful, step-by-step exploration program. With the successful completion of the Nicollet surveys in 1838-39, Abert determined that Nicollet should begin similar work west along the Oregon Trail-Platte River corridor. Because the precise location of South Pass on the Continental Divide in present-day Wyoming was uncertain—it might have been within the territorial limits of the Republic of Mexico—Abert did not consider the pass to be part of the expedition he had in mind. Nicollet was the obvious choice to lead the 1842 reconnaissance, but his failing health now made that impossible. Like so many others, Nicollet had been drawn to Frémont and saw him as both protégé and successor. It was Nicollet, not Benton, who urged Abert to send the young lieutenant west in the spring of 1842.

While Nicollet had enjoyed Abert's full confidence and was given broad powers to plan expeditions, the colonel was much less sure about Frémont. In late April 1842 Abert ordered Frémont to reconnoiter the Platte River "up to the head of the Sweetwater" and then, if time allowed, scout the Kansas River as well. Because those instructions did not include mention of South Pass, Benton urged Abert to extend the reach of Frémont's journey. In Benton's mind South Pass "may be considered the most striking and interesting point in the connection with the country of the Columbia River."[2] Abert was surely aware of Benton's political power, but at the same time he did not want to overload an untried expedition leader with too many missions. And there was the unresolved diplomatic-geographic question about the precise location of the pass. In an already highly charged atmosphere between the neighboring republics, it would do no good for soldier-explorers to go tramping into Mexican territory.

Even a quick look at Frémont's 1842 expedition along the Oregon Trail suggests the outlines for future trips. Frémont left St. Louis on May 2 with quite narrow instructions. Despite Benton's intervention, South Pass and crossing the Continental Divide was not part of the official plan. But once away from St. Louis Frémont exceeded his orders and went for the pass. Frémont was also fascinated by the latest technology, even if such devices were ill suited for demanding frontier travel. He purchased an inflatable India rubber boat and equipment to make daguerreotypes. The personnel on this and subsequent expeditions were distinctively Frémont's. While Lewis and Clark recruited most of their permanent party from the ranks of the army, Frémont preferred mountain men like Kit Carson and Alexis Godey along with the company of St. Louis voyageurs. The scientific world was the sole province of Frémont himself and his gifted cartographer, Charles Preuss. Frémont expeditions came to be part science, part adventure in a memorable mix of demanding travel, real suffering, and grand exhilaration.

During his first summer in the West, Frémont was more trail follower than pathfinder. The Oregon Trail-Platte River road over South Pass was already well known to trappers, merchants, and the first Oregon-bound overlanders. What stand out in that summer adventure were two emblematic episodes, each revealing something fundamental about Frémont and his age.

Having scouted South Pass in early August, Frémont and his men headed to the central chain of Wyoming's Wind River Range. On August 15 Frémont and a small party

John Charles Frémont ("The Pathfinder") and his wife and writing partner, Jessie Benton Frémont.

began to climb what he thought was "the highest peak of the Rocky Mountains." Frémont carried with him on the ascent two objects that represented his twin allegiances—a barometer and a specially made American flag. Once at the snowy crest of what is today Woodrow Wilson Peak, the adventurers "mounted the barometer in the snow of the summit, and fixing a ramrod in a crevice, unfurled the national flag to wave in the breeze where never flag waved before."[3] This was no ordinary flag but one emblazoned with an eagle holding arrows and a peace pipe in its claws. Later portrayed in a widely distributed lithograph, the image of bold Frémont with flag in hand on the spine of the continent seemed to embody all the exuberant nationalism of the time. But in a touch that must have pleased the literary sensibilities of Jessie Benton Frémont, this scene of science and empire was interrupted by the presence of a solitary bumblebee. Bees had long been thought by some writers to represent the spread of Euro-American settlement on the frontier. And now Frémont made the same point: "It was a strange place, an icy rock and the highest peak of the Rocky Mountains, for a lover of warm sunshine and flowers, and we pleased ourselves with the idea that he was the first of his species to cross the mountain barrier, a solitary pioneer to foretell the advance of civilization."[4] The barometer, the flag, and the bee; science, empire, and domestic civilization—each represented important aspects of Frémont's mission and the self-image of the nation.

If the young explorer felt proud of this mountaintop experience, what happened in the swirling current of the Sweetwater River was anything but triumphant. On August 24, with the expedition homeward bound, Frémont loaded important scientific records and instruments in his rubber boat for a foolhardy river run. In raging white water, the boat capsized, spilling into the river "books and boxes, bales of blankets, and scattered articles of clothing."[5] Frémont's original journals and many important botanical specimens were lost. As he confessed to botanist Dr. John Torrey some months later, the surviving samples were in so poor and confused a condition that "I am afraid you will find it almost impossible to fix localities from the labels."[6] What happened at the Sweetwater revealed a soldier-explorer all too eager to place his expedition in harms way, just to claim a bold gesture.

After returning to St. Louis in mid October, Frémont hurried to Washington, there to join Jessie. In the months that followed the Frémonts struggled to prepare an expedition report. The surviving botanical specimens were sent to Torrey while Preuss worked on a map of the Oregon Trail as far as South Pass. Neither John Charles nor Jessie expected that the expedition report would be a dry piece of writing aimed only at federal officials and scholars. What both sought was something readable, something both informative and entertaining directed at a wider audience. Hampered by the loss of his original journals and finding it difficult to write, Frémont began to dictate his report to Jessie. While this creative process can never be fully described, it does seem plain that Jessie became her husband's literary voice. And in later years she became her own voice as well. On March 1, 1845, Frémont submitted his finished report to Abert. As an exploration document it left much to be desired, but it did announce the presence of a soldier-explorer with a flair for publicity, self-advertisement, and the grand gesture. And at a time when such grand gestures drew public attention, Frémont was on the way to becoming both a western explorer and an authentic American celebrity.

Well before Frémont's return, Abert pursued his patient efforts to accomplish a comprehensive survey of the West. In the first months of 1843, with many in Congress calling for direct American action against Great Britain in the Oregon country, Abert began to plan a second western expedition. Early in March Benton wrote Abert urging that his son-in-law be sent "in the vicinity of the Rocky Mountains." While the Benton letter has not survived, Abert's reply has.[7] Adopting a conciliatory tone, he politely thanked Benton for his suggestions. Several days later Abert issued formal expedition orders to Frémont, orders that certainly had Benton's imprint on them.

Because Benton's March 7, 1843, letter to Abert has now vanished, it is not possible to know precisely what exploration strategies the senator had in mind. What has survived is the enclosure attached to the cover letter Abert sent to Frémont on March 10. In their definitive edition of the Frémont exploration records, Donald Jackson and Mary Lee Spence suggest that the enclosure with its plan was virtually a copy of what Benton had sent Abert just days before. A careful reading of those instructions reveals the imprint of Benton and his expansionist-minded congressional colleagues. Frémont was ordered to plot "the main forks of the Kansas River," then move to the headwaters of the Arkansas, tracing "the boundary between the United States and Mexico."[8] The most significant portion of the instructions proposed linking Frémont's overland exploration with the Pacific Ocean and Pacific Northwest surveys just completed by the navy's Lieutenant Charles Wilkes. Such a linkage would have appealed to Nicollet and Abert; it surely fit Benton's dream of an American presence on the Columbia. But the official instructions never sanctioned Frémont's return swing through Mexican California.

Abert envisioned the second Frémont expedition as yet another measured step in the army exploration of the West. But Benton, and probably Frémont, evidently could not be satisfied with Abert's cautious ways. Writing to Frémont just ten days after Abert's instructions were drafted, Benton offered his notion of how Frémont should present himself and who he represented. Because Frémont perhaps paid more attention to his father-in-law than his commanding officer, Benton's letter is worth quoting in full: "In the very important expedition which you are fitting out to the region beyond the *Rocky Mountains*, and to complete the gap in the Surveys between South Pass and the head of tidewater in the Columbia, the officer in command has to appear to the Indians as *the representative of the government*, and not as the officer of a bureau."[9]

Benton's letter was not only a slap at Abert, it was also a considerable stretching of Frémont's official orders. Urging the young explorer to consider himself on a diplomatic mission to the western tribes, Benton suggested that Frémont lay in an added supply of trade goods useful in formal negotiations. By May 1843 Frémont characterized his impending journey as "an expedition, military and geographical."[10] Meanwhile, Abert insisted that the trip was only "an expedition to gather scientific knowledge."[11]

This clash of views and objectives finally exploded in a now-famous and often misunderstood incident at the beginning of the expedition. Frémont decided that in addition to the usual supply of weapons required for such a journey he would also take along a lightweight mountain howitzer. When in early May 1843 he filed his request, army officers at the St. Louis arsenal proceeded to fill the requisition but also sent the paperwork to Abert. At the end of May, Abert wrote Frémont reminding him that "the object of the Department was a peaceable expedition" hardly requiring such ordnance.[12] Frémont had argued that the presence of hostile Indians made the howitzer essential for the expedition's very survival. Rejecting such reasoning, Abert declared: "If the condition of the Indians in the mountains is such to require your party to be so warlike in its equipment," it seemed plain that science would not be well served and the journey should be abandoned. At the same time, Abert wrote to both Jessie and Senator Benton, offering careful explanations for his decision and promising continued support for "a highly promising officer."[13]

Abert's May 22 letter to Frémont did not reach St. Louis until after the explorer's departure. Years later, in a *Century Magazine* article, Jessie fabricated a rather different and more dramatic story. She told her readers that she managed to delay Abert's letter, sending one of her own to hurry her explorer husband out of the hands of sinister forces. But it was the slowness of the post and Frémont's prompt departure from St. Louis that kept the howitzer as part of expedition baggage.

Gathering his usual party of mountain men and French voyageurs, Frémont left St. Louis on May 29 for what William H. Goetzmann has called a great "circumnavigation of the West."[14] The expedition's first objective was Fort St. Vrain on the South Platte River. In familiar Oregon Trail country, Frémont stayed south of the route he used in 1842, explaining that the expedition was scouting "a new road to Oregon and California, in a climate more genial."[15] In mid July, at Big Timber on the Smoky Hill River in present-day Kansas, Frémont paused to divide the expedition. He would press ahead while mountain man Thomas Fitzpatrick stayed with the slower-moving baggage train. In late July Frémont's advance party crossed the mountains at Cache la Poudre River near present-day Fort Collins, Colorado. After making his way across the Laramie Plain—"a continued and dense field of *artemisia*, which now entirely covered the country in such a luxuriant growth that it was difficult and laborious for a man on foot to force his way though, and nearly impracticable for our light carriages"—Frémont picked up the main stem of the Oregon Trail at the Sweetwater River.[16]

Centuries of geographic lore and more recent fur trapper experience all told of a vast interior lake somewhere in present-day Utah. As Frémont explained in late August 1843, "In our occasional conversations with the few old hunters who had visited the region, it had been a subject of frequent speculation; and the wonders they related were not the less agreeable because they were highly exaggerated and impossible."[17] Because Frémont prepared his report after the expedition, and his original journals have not survived, it is difficult to sort out what he knew in August 1843 from the more comprehensive view he had of the region many months later. What is plain is that Frémont's imagination was sparked by the possibility of exploring the Great Salt Lake and what he later named the Great Basin. From late August to mid September Frémont's party undertook a reconnaissance of the Great Salt Lake region. Reaching the lake on September 6, Frémont penned one of the most memorable and revealing passages in his report. Here, wrote the explorer, "the waters of the Inland Sea, stretch[ed] in still and solitary grandeur far beyond the limit of our vision." Describing the lake as "one of the great points of exploration," Frémont likened himself to Spanish explorer Vasco Nuñez de Balboa seeing the Pacific Ocean for the first time.[18] Frémont had once again packed along a rubber inflatable boat. Unaware that William H. Ashley's trappers had paddled around the lake in 1826, Frémont determined on a boat expedition around "this interior sea."[19]

Having completed his maritime adventure, Frémont headed toward his next objective—the Hudson's Bay Company outpost at Fort Hall on the Snake River in present-day

Idaho. Marching through the Bear River country on the way to Fort Hall, Frémont was impressed with the possibilities of the region. "The bottoms are extensive; water excellent; timber sufficient; the soil good, and well adapted to the grains and grasses suited to such an elevated region. A military post, and a civilized settlement, would be of great value here."[20] Mormon emigrants at Nauvoo in 1845-46, reading about a place Frémont described as "a bucolic region," found reason to point themselves toward so promising a place.

Frémont's expedition reached Fort Hall on September 19. After sending some expedition members back to St. Louis, the main party pointed itself toward the Grand Ronde near present-day LaGrande, Oregon. Ever alert to the possibilities for agricultural settlement, Frémont described the countryside in nearly Edenic terms. "A beautiful level basin, or mountain valley," the Grand Ronde was "covered with good grass, on a rich soil, abundantly watered, and surrounded by high and well-timbered mountains, and its name descriptive of its form—a great circle. It is a place—one of the few we have seen in our journey so far—where a farmer would delight to establish himself."[21]

In late October, with the westbound journey coming to a close, the Frémont expedition reached Whitman Mission, the trading post at Fort Walla Walla, and then pressed on to The Dalles on the Columbia River. On November 4 Frémont reached The Dalles and now considered his western journey complete. "Being now upon the ground explored by the South Sea expedition under Captain Wilkes, and having accomplished the object of uniting my survey with his, and thus presenting a connected exploration from the Mississippi to the Pacific," Frémont turned his attention to "objects" well beyond the scope of his original instructions.[22] After a brief visit to Fort Vancouver to meet with Hudson's Bay Company officer Dr. John McLoughlin, Frémont began to fashion a new exploration strategy for the homeward journey.

Colonel Abert neither envisioned nor sanctioned what Frémont now proposed—a great swing south from the Columbia, into Mexican California, and then east through present-day Nevada, Arizona, and Utah. In an entry from his published *Report* dated November 18, Frémont spelled out his plans for "a new route," a "great circuit to the South and southeast, and the exploration of the Great Basin between the Rocky mountains and the Sierra Nevada."[23] The explorer detailed three key exploration objectives: the location of Klamath Lake, the mapping of the ghost river known as the Buenaventura, and a reconnaissance of the southern reaches of the Rockies. The history of western exploration is filled with searches for ghost rivers. Lewis and Clark had great hopes for the Multnomah; the Caledonia played an important role in negotiations leading to the 1818 Treaty of Joint Occupation. But no phantom proved more tempting and more elusive than what the Spanish termed the Rio San Buenaventura. Drawing on eighteenth-century Spanish conjectures, many geographers and cartographers featured the Buenaventura as a great river highway south of the Columbia running from the Rockies to the Pacific. This was another part of the passage to India dream. In the 1820s fur trade explorers William H. Ashley, Peter Skene Ogden, and Jedediah Smith expended considerable time in futile searches for the

Buenaventura. While the mythical Buenaventura gradually vanished from the best contemporary maps, the idea of a water highway to the Pacific had lost none of its appeal. Thomas Hart Benton was one of those true believers and perhaps passed that piece of geographic faith on to Frémont. However, it is distinctly possible that a search for a ghost river was simply a pretext to reconnoiter lands held by the Mexican republic. Donald Jackson, Frémont's most recent and perceptive editor, pointedly observed that "Frémont's recurring journal entries about his search for the fabled river—written *after* the expedition— and his final conclusion that the river did not exist, seem almost like a deliberately introduced element to add continuity and suspense to the *Report*. It is hard to resist the suspicion that Jessie Benton Frémont's flair for the dramatic is somehow involved."[24]

Whatever the state of Frémont's geographic knowledge and the character of his real intentions, in late November the American expedition left The Dalles and headed south along the waters of the Deschutes River in central Oregon to find Klamath Lake. Frémont boldly proclaimed that his "projected line of return" would take the explorers into territories "a great part of it absolutely new to geographical, botanical, and geological science."[25] On December 10 Frémont believed he had found today's Upper Klamath Lake. Mistaken in his identification and confusing Klamath Marsh for the lake, Frémont then turned east into present-day Nevada. Struggling through difficult country in winter conditions, the explorer finally concluded that survival depended on turning west to cross the Sierra Nevada mountains and find safety in California. The change in plan, so Frémont reported, "was heard with joy by the people, and diffused new life throughout the camp."[26]

Frémont had stretched his orders in 1842 when he explored South Pass; his decision to winter in Mexican California came near to violating his instructions. There is no doubt that Frémont and his men could have spent a comfortable winter on either the Walker or Truckee rivers, countries with abundant food for his company and forage for expedition animals. Instead, he chose to risk a hazardous winter passage over the Sierra Nevada mountains, a decision that exposed his men to terrible privation. Historians continue to speculate about Frémont's political and imperial motives for this and his subsequent California adventure. The soldier-explorer could not have missed Benton's glowing words about America's Pacific destiny. And considering several entries in Charles Preuss's diary, it is possible that Frémont had decided to winter in California even before heading south from The Dalles.

After a harrowing passage over the Sierras by way of an unnamed and unidentified pass south of present-day Carson Pass (February 20, 1844), the explorers began their painful descent into the valley of the American River. Frémont's objective was Sutter's Fort on the banks of the Sacramento River. After the hardships of the mountain passage, California seemed a western paradise. Charles Preuss, not a man given to flights of gilded rhetoric, exclaimed: "One does not [often] see such sunrises and morning and evening glows." Comparing California to Italy and Greece, the usually grim cartographer pronounced the sky "as blue as forget-me-nots."[27] Frémont himself was equally enthralled with California, reminding us that the Golden State eventually became his chosen home

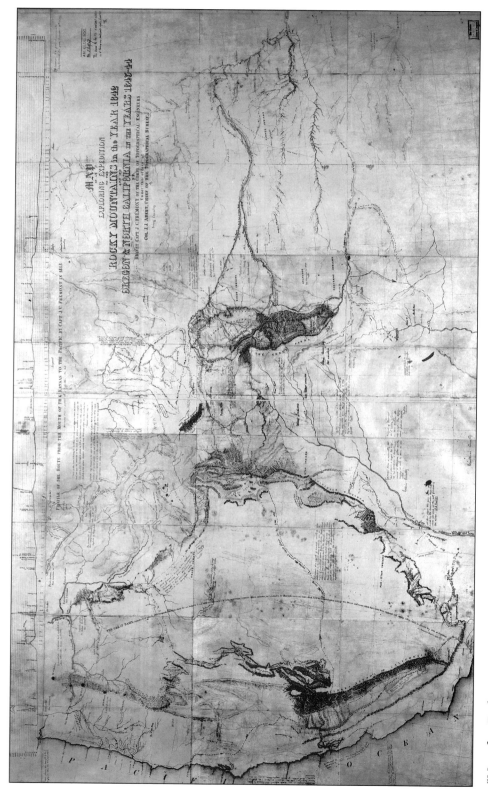

"Map of an Exploring Expedition to the Rocky Mountains in the Year 1842, and Oregon & North California in the Years 1843-44," by John C. Frémont and Charles Preuss, 1845.

place. Traveling toward Sutter's Fort, the explorer marveled at "the perpetual spring of the Sacramento."[28]

Frémont's expedition reached the fort on March 8, 1844, and remained until near the end of the month. After leaving Sutter, the Americans moved south through the San Joaquin Valley. Here again Frémont paused in his *Report* to describe California in the most glowing terms. "A lover of natural beauty can imagine with what pleasure we rode among those flowering groves, which filled the air with a light and delicate fragrance."[29] In mid April the expedition crossed the mountains at Oak Creek Pass, just south of the famed Tehachapi Pass. Assessing his party, Frémont described what must have seemed to his readers a romantic and exotic sight:

Our cavalcade made a strange and grotesque appearance: and it was impossible to avoid reflecting upon our position and composition in this remote solitude. Within two degrees of the Pacific Ocean; already far south of the latitude of Monterey; and still forced on the south by a desert [the Mojave Desert] on one hand, and a mountain range [the San Gabriel and San Bernardino Mountains] on the other; guided by a civilized Indian, attended by two wild ones from the Sierra; a Chinook from the Columbia; and our own mixture of American, French, German—all armed, half wild; four or five languages heard at once; above a hundred horses and mules, half wild; American, Spanish, and Indian dresses and equipments intermingled—such was our composition. Our march was a sort of procession. Scouts ahead, and on the flanks; a front and rear division; the pack animals, baggage, and horned cattle, in the center; and the whole stretching a quarter of a mile along our dreary path. In this form we journeyed; looking more like we belonged to Asia than to the United States.[30]

In late April the expedition finally rode northeast out of California and through the southern tip of present-day Nevada. From there Frémont pressed along the Old Spanish Trail. Guided by famed mountain man Joseph R. Walker, Frémont was bound for his second encounter with the Great Basin and the Great Salt Lake. Walker had been through the country in 1833-34; Frémont could not have asked for a better guide. But Walker did not keep Frémont and Preuss from making a fundamental geographical error. On May 24 the expedition reached Utah Lake. Frémont immediately assumed that the lake—actually a body of water separate from the Great Salt Lake—was an arm of the "Inland Sea." "We have now accomplished," so he claimed, "an object we had in view when leaving The Dalles of the Columbia."[31] This was also the moment to ponder the unique character of the Great Basin. Months before, Frémont had taken note of the conjectures and tales that had swirled around the basin and its mysterious geography. Its very existence seemed mythical. But now, having considered it, Frémont confidently declared, "The existence of the Basin is therefore an established fact."[32] It was a fact that deeply troubled him. Ever the optimist, Frémont believed in the West as the Garden of the World. Yet the basin as desert seemed undeniable. In a remarkable passage, Frémont captured some of his own confusion about so bewildering a place.

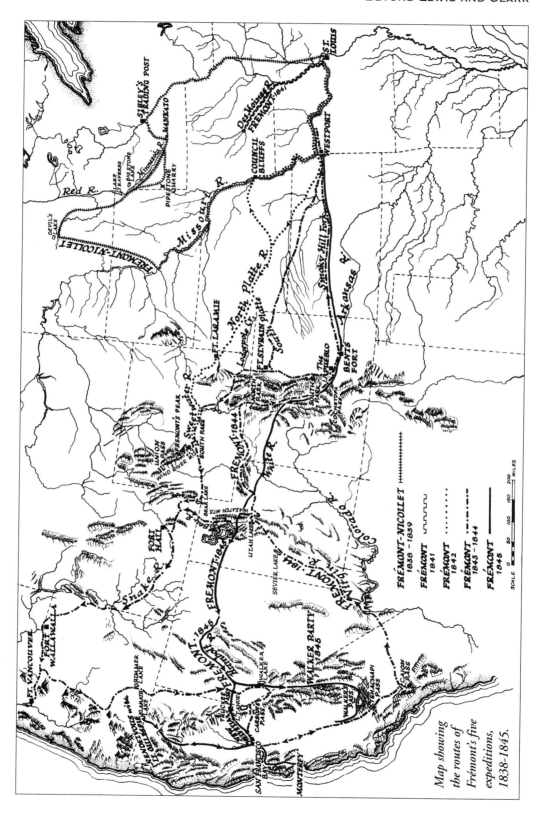

*Map showing
the routes of
Frémont's five
expeditions,
1838-1845.*

The whole idea of such a desert, and such a people [the Great Basin native inhabitants], is a novelty in our country, and excites Asiatic, not American ideas. Interior basins, with their own systems of lakes and rivers, and often sterile, are common enough in Asia; people still in the elementary state of families, living in deserts, with no other occupation than the mere animal search for food, might still be seen in that ancient quarter of the globe; but in America such things are new and strange, unknown and unsuspected, and discredited when related. But I flatter myself that what is discovered, though not enough to satisfy curiosity, is sufficient to excite it, and that subsequent explorations will complete what has been commenced.[33]

While Frémont did not return to St. Louis until August 6, in many ways his great western circuit ended at Utah Lake in the Great Basin. He had completed the loop, finished his epic voyage. The next time he would head west it would be more as an imperial adventurer than as a soldier-explorer. In the months that followed his return, Frémont was hailed as a national hero. The *Report of the Exploring Expedition to the Rocky Mountains in the Year 1842, and to Oregon and North California in the Years 1843-44* he and Jessie prepared was submitted on March 1, 1845, and was soon widely reprinted. Public interest was so great that Congress argued about whether former members might have their own supplies of the document. Commercial printings of the *Report* came in 1846; there was a London publication and a German translation the same year. Lewis and Clark had slipped from American memory. Now John Charles Frémont was rapidly becoming America's western pathfinder.

The phenomenal success the *Report* enjoyed quickly made Frémont a celebrity and national figure. On the eve of the Mexican War the young explorer seemed the ideal symbol for a rising American empire. And historians since have been quick to advance that understanding of the man who became Manifest Destiny's most visible symbol. But Frémont the symbol has come to obscure Frémont the explorer. John Charles Frémont may have become an inept politician and a failed entrepreneur in later years but in the early 1840s he was a talented, energetic western explorer. As a soldier-explorer Frémont made lasting contributions and suffered embarrassing disappointments. His contributions grew out of his own energy and intellect, tempered by the example of his mentor Nicollet. It was Nicollet who taught Frémont about serious exploration science seriously pursued. Frémont paid attention to scientific observation and the collecting of botanical specimens. But perhaps his greatest exploration contribution came in the maps prepared by Charles Preuss. Of all Preuss's maps none proved more influential than the one known as the Preuss-Frémont 1845 map. This cartographic landmark is properly titled "Map of an Exploring Expedition to the Rocky Mountains in the Year 1842 and to Oregon and North California in the Years 1843-44 by Brevet Captain J. C. Frémont of the Corps of Topographical Engineers." Distinguished cartographic scholar Carl I. Wheat maintained that the Frémont-Preuss 1845 map "changed the entire picture of the West and made a lasting contribution to cartography."[34] Unfolding

Frémont called on his fame as an explorer to aid in his
1856 run for president.

the map today, even the most casual observer is struck by three things: this map was built on actual travel experience; it is a "white space" map that depicts for the most part only those parts of the West seen by the Frémont expeditions; and it was founded on the best cartographic and surveying science available. For all those virtues, the map's most striking feature is an arc of print curving from Oregon to California that reads: "The Great Basin: diameter 11° of latitude, 10° of longitude: elevation above the sea between 4 and 5000 feet: surrounded by lofty mountains: contents almost unknown, but believed to be filled with rivers and lakes which have no communication with the sea, deserts and oases which have never been explored, and savage tribes, which no traveler has seen or described." As Donald Jackson writes in his notes on the 1845 map, it was "the right map at the right time."[35] The nation was now ready to act on the information and vision expressed in the map.

Frémont the soldier-explorer wanted to be remembered as a man of science. But as other soldier-explorers were to learn, the precise needs of science were often at odds with the daily demands and twists and turns of an exploration journey. Nothing illustrates better the troubled course of Frémont's exploration science than the unhappy history of his botanical specimens. Samples from the first expedition were either lost or damaged in the Sweetwater River rubber boat fiasco. Many of those from the second expedition also suffered an unfortunate fate. Writing to botanist John Torrey in September 1844 Frémont reported that plants collected on the journey from Fort Hall to Upper California were "entirely lost by a fall of a mule. The animal was killed and the bales could not be recovered."[36] But the greatest blow fell on the night of July 13-14, 1844, when a flood on the Kansas River soaked and ruined the remaining collections. "I have never had," Frémont lamented, "a severer trial of my fortitude."[37]

Like Zebulon Montgomery Pike, John Charles Frémont has not fared well in American memory. The Pathfinder was once the army's and the nation's most famous explorer. He is often a mere name in a textbook, now reshadowed by Lewis and Clark. Frémont's life was a strange combination of serious science, boyish enthusiasm, and a penchant for bold, sometimes impetuous deeds. He saw himself as both scientist and adventurer, a romantic traveler in search of the exotic, and a dedicated, clear-eyed expansionist.

Always something of an outsider in army circles because he was not a West Point graduate, Frémont's celebrity status made him even more suspect by those soldier-explorers who endorsed Abert's cautious exploration program. But no matter how much he tried Abert's patience, Frémont had his commanding officer's confidence. What ended the explorer's military career were not his exploration failures and acts of insubordination but a rancorous court-martial that grew out of political and personal controversies with General Stephen Watts Kearny in California after the Mexican War.

The troubles between Kearny and Frémont began in January 1847 when the general and his troops marched from San Diego to Los Angeles. Frémont, now signing his letters with the grand title "Military Commander of the Territory of California," had established himself in Los Angeles as the ranking military officer and civil authority. Frémont

went so far as to negotiate a peace treaty with Mexican officials, a responsibility that
clearly belonged to Kearny. For nearly four months Frémont disregarded direct orders
from his commanding officer. Finally exasperated by the Pathfinder's presumptions, Kearny
ordered Frémont back to Washington to face a general court martial. The charges against
Frémont were daunting: disobeying direct orders from a superior officer, mutiny, and
conduct prejudicial to military discipline. The Frémont trial dragged out from early November 1847 to late January 1848. Among those who testified against Frémont was William H. Emory, something that Frémont and Senator Benton never forgot. The panel of
regular army officers (including Major Stephen H. Long) returned a guilty verdict. President Polk, sensing the political consequences of such a decision, adroitly upheld the
court's finding while canceling Frémont's dismissal. Knowing that his military career was
finished, Frémont resigned in mid February 1848. No soldier-explorer had risen so rapidly or fallen so swiftly.

The Frémonts made exploration reports into popular literature. American audiences
eager for stories of adventure and discovery in remote and exotic places found their hero
in Frémont. Nurtured by a swelling nationalism, Frémont seemed to embody the expan-
siveness that some called "Young America." In him empire, the romance of the West, and
the life of the mind all seemed to come together. And then it all fell apart—at least for
John Charles and Jessie. After 1844 there would be three more western expeditions, the
end of the military career, ill-fated political and business ventures, and a slow descent into
relative obscurity. That Frémont the Pathfinder would die estranged from his wife, alone
in a dismal New York City rooming house seemed unimaginable in the glorious haze of
the 1840s.

Chapter

6

MANIFEST DESTINY AND THE SOLDIER-EXPLORERS

In 1845, the same year that Congress authorized publication of Frémont's *Report*, New York journalist John L. O'Sullivan wrote an editorial for his newspaper that seemed to capture all the empire-building energies and anxieties of the moment. It is, so O'Sullivan proclaimed, "the right of our manifest destiny to overspread and to possess the whole continent which providence has given us for the development of the great experiment in liberty and federated self-government."[1] It was not the first time that O'Sullivan had used the words "manifest destiny," but now in the midst of the debate over the future of Oregon as well as mounting tensions with Mexico on the issue of Texas, the phrase and the ideas behind it seemed to take on extra force and meaning. And for many, soldier-explorers like Frémont appeared the very manifestation of that destiny.

The ideas and passions behind O'Sullivan's sweeping declaration had been present in American life for centuries. The notion of one nation or people chosen by God or providence to carry out a special mission in a wilderness place found early expression in the works of seventeenth-century Puritan writers like William Bradford and John Winthrop. In his history of the Pilgrim colony, Bradford identified England as the nation chosen by God to first receive and then spread "the light of the gospel" in a world covered by "the gross darkness of popery."[2] John Winthrop's 1630 lay sermon, entitled "A Model of Christian Charity," made that religious mission even more plain. Winthrop declared that the Massachusetts Bay colony was to be "a Citty upon a hill."[3] Puritan writers and preachers did not directly link their sense of divine mission to territorial expansion, but the implication was clear enough, especially when English settlers cast their eyes on lands occupied by Native Americans. Those faithful who lived in the city on the hill were a people set apart, chosen by God to pursue an errand into the wilderness.

By the first years of the new American republic, what had been defined as a sacred project was rapidly becoming a civic, secular one. The Puritan sense of mission was transferred from a chosen religious people to an elect nation. William Henry Drayton, South Carolina planter and jurist, made plain in 1776 the territorial extent of that mission. "The

Almighty," he insisted, "has made choice of the present generation to erect an American empire."[4] A decade later, at the end of the Revolution, American geographer Jedediah Morse confidently predicted a time in the not-distant future "when the *AMERICAN EMPIRE* will comprehend millions of souls, west of the Mississippi."[5] In the newspaper war over the Louisiana Purchase, the *New York Evening Post* presented the case for a rising American empire of continental dimensions. "It belongs of *right* to the United States to regulate the future destiny of North America. The country is *ours*; ours is the right to its rivers and to all the sources of future opulence, power, and happiness."[6]

As a distinctive American nationalism emerged after the War of 1812, no public figure gave clearer expression to the core ideas of Manifest Destiny than Secretary of State John Quincy Adams. In 1818, during negotiations with Great Britain over the future of the Oregon country, Adams told crown officials that the West was "our natural dominion in North America."[7] Five years later, with Oregon still on his mind, Adams wrote American ambassador Richard Rush, offering a classic statement of the divine geography that determined the extent of the American empire. European nations should understand, so Adams insisted, that "the finger of Nature" pointed the American republic to the shores of the Pacific.[8] In a long entry in his diary on the future of the American nation, Adams predicted that "the world shall be familiarized with the idea of considering our proper dominion to be the continent of North America."[9]

What came to be called Manifest Destiny was never a comprehensive national ideology with a single leader speaking in one voice. Rather, it was a collection of ideas—some religious, some political, some geographic—about the shape of the American nation and the continent. Some voices in the Manifest Destiny shouting match were overtly racist, declaring that "darker peoples" had to give way before "superior Anglo-Saxons." Others called for the extension of American political institutions and the blessings of Protestant Christianity to those "still living in darkness." Some linked territorial expansion to personal economic gain and national prosperity. Finally, some, like Congressman Francis Baylies, put it all in terms of demographic inevitability. "Our natural boundary is the Pacific Ocean. The swelling tide of our population must and will roll on until that mighty ocean interposes its waters, and limits our territorial empire."[10] However defined and expressed, Manifest Destiny both reflected what historical geographer D. W. Meinig has called "the outward movement" and at the same time justified it in the name of religion, science, geography, and political idealism. In this chorus of voices one thing was plain: the United States had a western future. The uncertainty was whether God or Nature or human conquest would usher in that future. But however that future was defined and whoever brought it into being, Abert and his soldier-explorers embraced a larger America and understood themselves as agents in its making.

Chapter

7

SOLDIER-EXPLORERS AND THE MARCH INTO MEXICO

*W*hile advocates of a continental United States might have believed that expansion was inevitable, the West in the early 1840s was more like suspect terrain—a place where rival nations and peoples jockeyed for power and place. From the vantage point of the War Department, there seemed two places where conflict might erupt. One of those was the Pacific Northwest, where the boundary dispute between the United States and Great Britain had simmered since the first Joint Occupation Treaty in 1818. The second possible arena for war was the Southwest, especially in the disputed boundary region between the new state of Texas and the Republic of Mexico. Bernard DeVoto once described 1846—the year the Mexican War began—as "the year of decision." But for Colonel Abert and other military officers, the real year of decision came in 1845. Surveying the western landscape with an eye to future battlefields, it was plain that the army knew the Oregon country terrain reasonably well, thanks to the Wilkes and Frémont expeditions. But in the Southwest, military planners knew little more than what was available from the Pike report and various commercially printed maps. If the soldier-explorers of the Corps of Topographical Engineers were needed anywhere in 1845, it was on the edges of two poorly defined empires—the United States of America and the United States of Mexico.

In the spring of 1845 the War Department sent three expeditions into the West and Southwest. While these were principally military reconnaissance probes, all involved topographical engineers as scientific observers and cartographers. Colonel Stephen Watts Kearny led the first of these. Commanding five companies of the First Dragoons, Kearny left Fort Leavenworth on May 18 and followed the Oregon Trail to Fort Laramie. After a council with a band of Brulé Teton Sioux, the expedition scouted as far as South Pass before heading south along the Front Range of the Rockies in present-day Colorado. At Bent's Fort the Dragoons rode east, returning to Fort Leavenworth in late August. Kearny's topographical engineer was Lieutenant William B. Franklin, a recent West Point graduate.

Because the Dragoons moved so quickly—covering 2,200 miles in 99 days—Franklin had little time for anything other than the most basic cartography. But his map, based largely on Frémont and Preuss, did contain new information about the terrain between the Platte and the Arkansas. While Franklin was more than just along for the ride, Kearny plainly understood his expedition in military—not scientific—terms. He rode out of Fort Leavenworth to show the flag along a vital transcontinental highway and to impress plains Indians with the power of their Great Father. And all of this was a message not lost on officials in either London or Mexico City.[1]

While many senior army officers like Kearny had little use for the scientific side of Abert's exploration program, few doubted the strategic value of the maps and terrain reports that came from the soldier-explorers. The second army expedition sent west in 1845 was the most complex and ultimately the most controversial. Almost immediately after returning home from his second western expedition, John Charles Frémont began to plan a third. In a private letter to botanist John Torrey dated September 15, 1844, Frémont disclosed his plan to return to the West in April 1845. Swearing Torrey to secrecy, Frémont seemed to imply that he might be in California by the fall of the year. If Frémont, and perhaps Benton, had such a scheme in mind, the news escaped Abert and the War Department.

Early in 1845, as tensions between the United States and Mexico mounted over the issue of Texas annexation, Abert began to fashion quite different plans for Frémont. What the colonel had in mind was a limited scientific-military tour in the region of the Arkansas and Red River, and the boundary between Mexico and the United States. In a remarkable portion of his instructions to Frémont, Abert explicitly limited both the geographic range and the exploration strategy for the Pathfinder's third expedition. "Long journeys to determine isolated geographical points are scarcely worth the time and the expense which they occasion; the efforts of Captain Frémont will therefore be more particularly directed to the geography of localities within a reasonable distance of Bent's Fort, and of the streams which run east from the Rocky Mountains, and he will so time his operations, that his party will come in during the present year."[2]

In the months that followed, as Frémont continued to sort out affairs from his second expedition, plans went ahead for the third. Abert approved the addition of a "Botanical Colorist" for the expedition, allowed expansion of the expedition's personnel, and granted Frémont's request to detail a separate detachment to explore "regions South of the Arkansas." Topographical engineers Lieutenants James W. Abert (Colonel Abert's son) and William G. Peck were added to the expedition for that duty. In March 1845 Congress passed a joint resolution to annex Texas; Mexico promptly broke off diplomatic relations with the United States. And swirling around all of this were the expansionist dreams of the newly elected president, James K. Polk.

The stories of Frémont's adventure in California and his role in the Bear Flag Revolt have been often told. Despite years of painstaking research, historians have still not found the secret letter of instructions that Frémont claimed he carried from Benton. In his published *Memoirs*, the explorer insisted that he was directed "to extend the survey west and southwest to the examination of the great ranges of the Cascade and the Sierra Nevada, so as to ascertain the lines of communication through the mountains to the ocean in that latitude."[3] What is clear is that sometime after leaving Westport in late June 1845 and reaching California that fall, Frémont became less an explorer than an unofficial, free-wheeling agent for American expansion. Although he talked about scientific exploration in letters to Jessie, he kept no journal and never filed any official exploration report.

While Frémont's California adventure moved him out of the world of exploration and into a quagmire of international politics and personal intrigue, Lieutenants Abert and Peck conducted a valuable tour of the country south of Bent's Fort and then east through present-day northeastern New Mexico, the Texas panhandle, and central Oklahoma. The Abert-Peck expedition, guided partway by mountain-man Thomas Fitzpatrick, left Bent's Fort in August hoping among other things to sort out the puzzle of the Red River headwaters. They were moving into what historian John Miller Morris has aptly called a "zone of uncertainty."[4]

While the soldier-explorers failed in that mission, the report Lieutenant Abert prepared was a model for its genre. Abert had a keen eye for detail, accurately describing plants, animals, and the landscape. And he proved an artist as well. Moving quickly through what he described as "regions of deep interest to the naturalist," Abert regretted that he could not pause to make "suitable collections of the fauna, avia, flora etc."[5] What he did, however, was write prose that was both precise and colorful.

His language was matched by considerable artistic skill. Drawing was an essential part of a West Point education, and Abert proved a talented artist. His paintings of native peoples, landscapes, and wildlife remain remarkable examples of exploration art. Abert's published *Report*, his paintings, and Peck's map combined travel narrative with scientific observation and imperial ambition. Like the Frémonts at their best, these young soldier-explorers put the West on paper and made that West seem a natural part of the United States.

In 1845 the War Department sent three expeditions to reconnoiter the edges of empire. As the year drew to a close, events moved swiftly toward some kind of collision between the United States and Mexico. Both were republics; both had imperial ambitions; and both had political leaders willing to go to the brink of war to fulfill what they thought were national destinies. Tensions between the two neighbors over the international border dramatically increased when newly elected president James K. Polk rejected Mexican claims that the border was the Neuces River, insisting that the Rio Grande was the proper boundary. Between those two rivers was a strip of contested territory some 150 miles across. Polk not only demanded that Mexico accept the Rio Grande boundary, he also ordered American troops into the disputed zone. By March 1846 American forces were camped opposite Matamoros while the navy blockaded the port. It seems plain that Polk hoped to tempt Mexican forces into firing the first shot, thereby giving the United States reason to declare war. When that did not happen, Polk was ready to ask Congress for a declaration of war based on Mexico's failure to pay debts owed to American citizens.

On May 9, 1846, Polk's cabinet approved a draft declaration of war to be presented to Congress. But as fate would have it, the cabinet's decision was overtaken by events in the Southwest. Later that afternoon word came of an armed clash on April 25 between Mexican and American forces. Polk could now claim that Mexico had "invaded our territory and shed American blood on American soil." Congressional opposition to war was weak and divided. On May 13, 1846, the United States declared war on the Republic of Mexico.

William H. Emory.

For the soldier-explorers of the Corps of Topographical Engineers, the Mexican War was their first combat experience, and it laid the foundation for their most productive decade. The two great exploration enterprises of the 1850s—the United States-Mexican Boundary Survey and the Pacific Railroad Surveys—were the direct result of territorial acquisitions at the end of the war. Those surveys both defined western boundaries and described the lands within them. The Mexican War changed the political and cultural map of North America. Soldier-explorers soon found themselves marching into that new West and making those maps.

In today's book of American memory the name William H. Emory finds almost no place. While John Charles Frémont—once famous—has slipped into near obscurity, William Hemsley Emory—important but never famous—has escaped us almost entirely. But perhaps more than any other soldier-explorer of the age, Emory exemplified the topographical engineer ideal. An experienced explorer and frontier traveler, he was as much at home in the mountains of New Mexico as in the War Department's cartographic drafting rooms. Emory rode with Kit Carson, corresponded with scientists like John Torrey and George Engelmann, and negotiated with Mexican officials throughout the tortured course of the United States-Mexican Boundary Survey. To follow Emory's tracks is to trace the golden years of army exploration.

Born into a powerful Maryland landholding family, Emory enjoyed all the privileges his social standing could afford. Well-educated and with a taste for riding and fox hunting, Emory got his appointment to West Point in 1823 from family friend John C. Calhoun. As a member of the Class of 1831, Emory received a superb education and joined a prominent social circle that included Jefferson Davis, Henry Clay, Jr., and Joseph E. Johnson. The love of fast horses and daring exploits gave Emory his lifelong nickname—"Bold Emory." The young officer enjoyed influential friends and, like Frémont, he married well. His wife, Matilda Wilkins Bache, was not only the great-granddaughter of Benjamin Franklin but also the daughter of Alexander D. Bache, director of the government's Coast and Geodetic Survey. It was through the Bache family that Emory made a whole series of important political friendships.

But it would be a mistake to think of "Bold Emory" as just one more young Southerner bent on recreating the Age of Chivalry in the American army. It was science—especially what we call the earth sciences—that captured Emory's mind and imagination. Widely read in everything from astronomy and archaeology to geology and zoology, Emory became part of the intellectual circle that included notable scholars at Princeton, Harvard, and the Smithsonian Institution. Not only did he correspond with researchers like Torrey, Engelmann, and Spencer F. Baird—this solder-explorer, in the words of William H. Goetzmann, found a regular place in "the yearly conclaves of the American Association for the Advancement of Science."[6] Emory's most important assignments before the Mexican War—a post in the Northeast Boundary Survey of 1843-44 and the preparation of a Texas map in 1844—clearly indicated the cast of mind for a westering soldier-explorer.

Not many American military units have had a grander title and a more demanding mission with fewer resources than Stephen Watts Kearny's "Army of the West." With less than two thousand troops—some of them volunteers—Kearny was commanded to conquer New Mexico and then move on to occupy California. On June 5, 1846, Lieutenant Emory was ordered to organize a topographical engineer detachment and then rendezvous with Kearny at Fort Leavenworth. As Emory later recalled, he had not much more than twenty-four hours in Washington "to collect the instruments and other conveniences for such an expedition."[7] While Colonel Abert did not spell out in detail the specific mission, Emory understood that his party "should be employed in collecting data that would give the government some idea of the regions traversed."[8] Considering the proposed geographic range of Kearny's mission, this would be no simple task. Joining Emory were two experienced soldier-explorers—Lieutenants Abert and Peck. Emory's detachment also included a third topographical engineer, Lieutenant W. H. Warner. As if to reemphasize the scientific nature of what was really a wartime reconnaissance, Emory also had the services of statistician Norman Bestor and landscape artist John Mix Stanley. Emory certainly knew that in wartime his exploration mission might be at odds with his purely military duties. In a revealing note at the beginning of his official report, he wrote the following:

This [his supply of scientific instruments] was quite sufficient for all the objects appertaining directly to our military wants, but insufficient for the organization and outfit of a party intended for exploration. In submitting the following notes, they should be received as observations made at intervals snatched from other duties, and with an expedition whose movements were directed by other considerations than those which would influence the views and conveniences of an explorer.[9]

Emory need not have apologized; his *Notes of a Military Reconnaissance from Fort Leavenworth, in Missouri, to San Diego, in California* remains an example of army exploration writing at its best.

The Army of the West left Fort Leavenworth at the end of June 1846 and made camp outside Bent's Fort a month later. By 1846 the route was so well-known that Emory did not begin his formal report until the troops marched south in the first week of August. Guided by Thomas Fitzpatrick, Kearny's army took the familiar trail over Raton Pass. While tensions mounted over a possible encounter with Mexican forces led by General Manuel Armijo, American troops entered and occupied Santa Fe on August 18 without meeting any organized resistance. After consolidating his hold on Santa Fe, Kearny determined to continue his passage to California. On September 25 the Army of the West, including Emory's fourteen-man topographical detachment, rode south down the Rio Grande Valley past present-day Albuquerque and Socorro. That march was dramatically interrupted on October 6 when the expedition met Kit Carson. Sent hurrying east by Frémont with news from California, Carson reported that the "country had surrendered without a blow, and that the American flag floated in every port."[10] As events later proved, it was an overly optimistic evaluation of the military situation.

Encouraged by this news, Kearny sent part of his command back to Santa Fe while the rest of his force, including Emory's unit, followed Carson west along the Gila River through present-day south-central New Mexico and Arizona. At the confluence of the Gila and Colorado rivers the expedition made a difficult desert passage and then struggled over the Sierra Madre Mountains into California. Frémont's claim that the entire country had surrendered proved tragically wrong at the Battle of San Pascual (December 6, 1846) when Kearny's exhausted troops suffered heavy casualties at the hands of Mexican lancers. "Bold Emory" proved worthy of his nickname when he rescued Kearny from certain death. Emory's epic southwestern journey did not end until later in December when American troops occupied San Diego. Only then could he report that "my work as a topographical engineer may be considered to end at this place."[11]

The bare outlines of Emory's journey only hint at its importance and the quality of his published *Notes.* Like the Frémonts, Emory instinctively knew how to tell a good story. His descriptions of travel are among the best in exploration literature. In the Peloncillos Mountains of the Gila country Emory wrote: "The metallic clink of spurs, and the rattling of the mule shoes, the high, black peaks, the deep dark ravines, and the unearthly looking cacti,

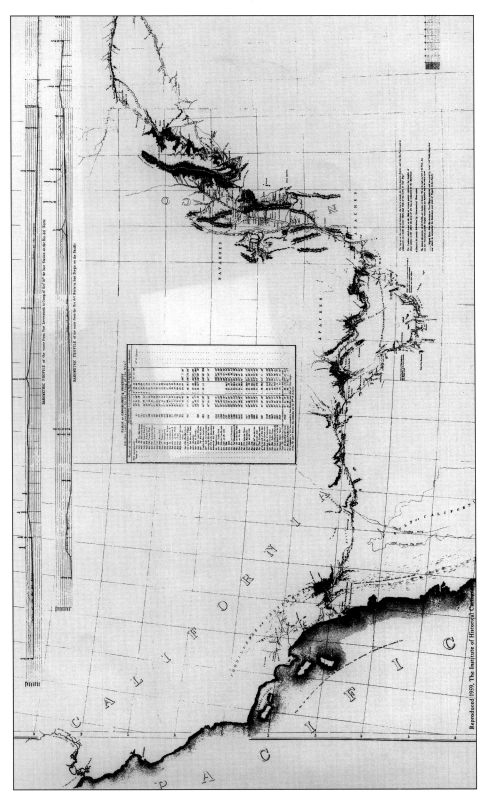

Map showing William H. Emory's 1846 Southwest

which stuck out from the rocks like the ears of Mephistophiles, all favored the idea that we were now treading on the verge of the regions below."[12] Emory knew firsthand the rigors of desert travel, describing in painful detail the thirst and exhaustion that swept the ranks of the Army of the West. And he also knew that such travel was often at odds with his exploration goals. Studying the mountains around Raton Pass, he wrote "there may be mineral wealth in these mountains, but its discovery must be left to some explorer not attached to the staff of an army making forced marches into an enemy's country."[13] Later in the journey, when he wanted to examine the country around present-day Socorro, New Mexico, Emory again confronted the dilemma of the soldier-explorer in wartime. "But onward for California was the word, and he who deviated from the trail of the army must expect a long journey for his jaded beast and several days' separation from his baggage. We were not an exploring expedition; war was the object."[14]

Despite the rigors of constant travel, Emory did not fail to record and evaluate what Jefferson once called "the face of the country." Conditioned by a Maryland childhood and years of East Coast experience, Emory saw western landscapes through eastern eyes. For him, the Southwest was "weird and mysterious-looking."[15] In the Gila country, surrounded by the remains of now-abandoned Indian villages, Emory wrote his most compelling description of a world so unlike the country he called home. "Strolling over the hills alone, in pursuit of seed and geological specimens, my thoughts went back to the States, and when I turned from my momentary aberrations, I was struck most forcibly with the fact that not one object in the whole view, animal, vegetable or mineral, had anything in common with the products of any State in the Union, with the single exception of the cottonwood."[16] Ever the scientist, Emory speculated on the powerful forces that shaped so strange a place. Reflecting recent debates among geologists, Emory sided with those who saw the continent shaped by the gradual forces of erosion rather than sudden, catastrophic events. As William H. Goetzmann writes, such views put Emory "among the most advanced scientific thinkers of his time."[17]

The New Mexico country—Emory never used the word "Arizona"—might have been strange and perhaps even unsettling, but the soldier-explorer never doubted that it had a place in the American empire. His report is filled with suggestions about the shape of the regional future. Well before John Wesley Powell pointed out the significance of aridity in the West, Emory declared that "in no part of this vast tract can the rains of Heaven be relied upon, to any extent, for the cultivation of the soil. The earth is destitute of trees, and in great part also of any vegetation whatever."[18] Farming could flourish only in the river bottoms; Southerners need not bring their slaves to such a country since the cost of transportation alone would outweigh any profit. This was an arid landscape but not a country without a future. In one remarkable section of the report, Emory captured all the sense of possibility that swirled around the lands conquered during the Mexican War:

New Mexico, although its soil is barren, and its resources limited, unless the gold mines should, as is probable, be more extensively developed hereafter, and the culture of the grape

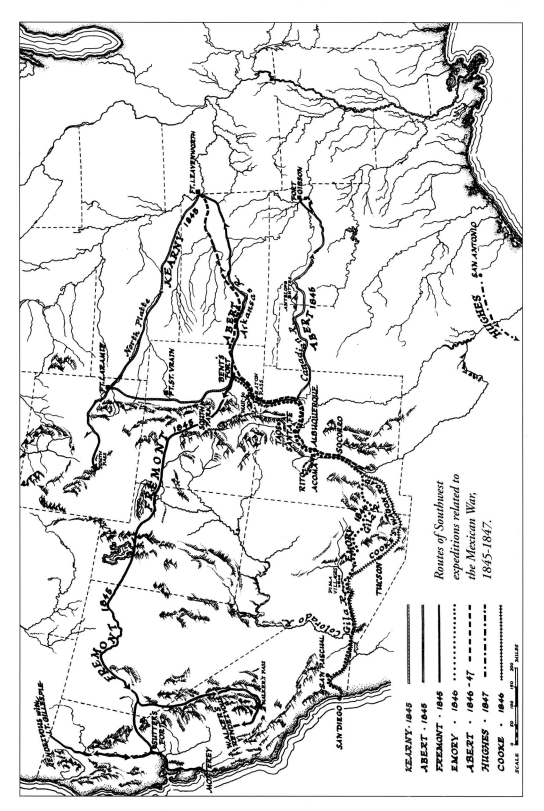

Routes of Southwest
expeditions related to
the Mexican War,
1845–1847.

KEARNY · 1845
ABERT · 1845
FREMONT · 1845
EMORY · 1846
ABERT · 1846-47
HUGHES · 1847
COOKE · 1846

SCALE 0 50 100 150 200 MILES

enlarged, is, from its position, in a commercial and military aspect, an all-important military possession for the United States. The road from Santa Fe to Fort Leavenworth presents few obstacles for a railway, and, if it continues as good to the Pacific, will be one of the routes to be considered, over which the United States will pass immense quantities of merchandise into what may become, in time, the rich and populous States of Sonora, Durango, and Southern California.[19]

Railroads, gold mines, and vineyards—here was a future promising enough for any ambitious American entrepreneur.

Emory the empire builder embraced what he thought was a promising American future in the Southwest. Emory the scientific explorer was fascinated by the Southwest's distant past. Like many other well-read Americans, his imagination was fired by accounts of ancient civilizations in John L. Stephens's, *Incidents of Travel in Central America, Chiapas, and Yucatan* (1841) and William H. Prescott's *The Conquest of Mexico* (1843). These books offered a vision of an America as ancient as any civilization in Europe, something that appealed to Emory's cultural patriotism as well as his scientific bent. While he always made careful observations about those native peoples like the Maricopas, Pimas, and Apaches along the route of march, it was the prospect of studying "lost civilizations" that captured his imagination. In ruined towns like Pecos in the Gila River country, Emory stood at what William H. Goetzmann has called "the crude beginning of American anthropological and archaeological studies in the West."[20]

Emory' slim report and the important map that accompanied it proved a treasure trove of information about the Southwest. The botanical specimens he did manage to collect went to John Torrey who enumerated one new genus and eighteen new species. No southwestern traveler could escape the presence of cacti. Emory sent his cactus samples to Dr. George Engelmann for study and analysis. Emory carried on a lively correspondence about Native American history and cultures with the redoubtable Albert Gallatin. Once one of Jefferson's ablest exploration advisors, Gallatin was still involved in the business of exploring some forty years after Lewis and Clark. Gallatin not only consulted with Emory and Frémont but also prepared the first comprehensive map of North American Indian languages. Perhaps Emory would have insisted that the most important accomplishment of the 1846 journey was his map. Built on more than two thousand observations and firsthand experience, the map offered the first accurate depiction of large parts of present-day New Mexico and Arizona.

Chapter

8

MARKING BOUNDARIES, MAKING TRACKS

No single armed conflict more completely changed the political outlines and cultural future of western North America than the Mexican War. The Republic of Mexico lost over one million square miles of its territory; the United States became a continental nation with vast new territories and an empire fronting on the Pacific. New boundaries sliced through lands and lives, redefining cultural identities and national loyalties. None of this was the product of some inevitable destiny or special American genius. At every step along the way—both before and after the war—there were unexpected twists and surprising turns. But at war's end North America had experienced a geopolitical transformation unprecedented in the nineteenth century. When added to the resolution of the Oregon Question with Great Britain in 1846 and the discovery of gold in California in 1848, all signs pointed to an American century in the West.

In the decade after its creation in 1838, the Corps of Topographical Engineers matured as a professional, self-confident group of soldier-explorers. Guided by Colonel Abert's comprehensive vision of western exploration, the topographical engineers produced maps and reports of growing significance to an expanding nation. Service in the Mexican War demonstrated that soldier-explorers like Emory were both men of science and men at arms. But the greatest challenge for the corps came in the decade after 1848. In those years the personnel and resources of the soldier-explorers would be tested in two of the American West's most demanding and complex exploration enterprises.

The Treaty of Guadalupe Hidalgo (signed on February 2, 1848) ended hostilities between the two nations and began to make clear just how much one had lost and the other had gained. But this was no ordinary treaty made to simply end a war and return lands and lives to the status quo antebellum. As historical geographer D. W. Meinig writes, "The Treaty of Guadalupe Hidalgo undertook a comprehensive redefinition of the geopolitical relations between the United States of America and the Republic of Mexico."[1] The engine for that redefinition was the new boundary between the two nations. Article Five of the treaty stipulated that boundary commissions from both nations would "run and mark the said Boundary...to designate...the line with due precision, upon authoritative maps, and to establish upon the ground landmarks which shall show the limits of the Republics."[2]

From the distance of Washington, D.C., or Mexico City, the language of Article Five sounded reassuringly precise and scientific. Trained surveyors would do their work and settle once and for all the contentious border problems that had brought the neighbors to war. As if to emphasize how disinterested the whole process would be, negotiators appended two copies of John Disturnell's "Map of the United Mexican States...constructed according to the Best Authorities" to the treaty draft. In reality, the Disturnell map was anything but authoritative. It was filled with imprecise locations and geographic misconceptions. Perhaps most telling, the two copies included in the draft treaty differed one from the other. Treaty language based on Disturnell was bound to spark diplomatic trouble and cause field surveyors endless confusion. The issue, as both American and Mexican diplomats and surveyors soon discovered, was not simply where to place the "great line." The enduring questions were ones of territory and access to the Pacific. Arguments about the latitudes of San Diego and El Paso proved more than disputes about survey mathematics; they came to represent national honor and each country's sense of the future.

The United States-Mexican Boundary Survey became the Corps of Topographical Engineers first great challenge after the Mexican War. The boundary commissions established by the American government were odd creatures with deeply troubled institutional lives. The commissions had both civilian and military employees. Under the general direction of the State Department and later the Department of the Interior, commissioners and surveyors were sometimes chosen for reasons of political patronage rather than administrative skill or scientific training. Working in the field, army topographical engineers found that the chain of command had uncertain—and often broken—links. Soldier-explorers were frequently at odds with their civilian counterparts, slowing the entire process and sometimes bringing it to a complete halt. Little wonder that the survey's field work, begun in July 1849, did not end until October 1855.

In many ways the boundary survey has two histories: a tumultuous story running through four separate commissions, and its accomplishments in creating the first comprehensive, scientific area survey of the border country between the United States and Mexico. The first story—its events and personalities—is by far the more colorful. Throughout the life of the survey, the American boundary commissions were home to all sorts of shenanigans, personal betrayals, political infighting, physical violence, and episodes of just plain foolishness. All of this was acted out by a remarkable cast of hard-working surveyors, political hacks, incompetent administrators, and sometimes-quarrelsome army engineers. While the Mexican survey commission was characterized by stability, competence, and personnel continuity, the American story was anything but that.

Perhaps it was an omen of things to come that the first American commissioner died before being confirmed in office. His successor was John B. Weller, an Ohio politician and the choice of the Polk administration. Texan Andrew B. Gray was named surveyor; Emory was appointed "Chief Astronomer and Commander of the Escort." Two other topographical engineers also joined the commission. As directed by the treaty, the boundary commissioners met in San Diego in July 1849 to begin work on the San Diego-Gila River portion of the survey. No sooner had work Emory described as "dreary and thankless" begun than it dissolved in a sea of controversy and personal bickering.[3] Funding was short and vital personnel slipped away to join the California gold rush. And there was the constant drumbeat of criticism from Washington. No boundary commission could ever be free from political debate, and the Weller commission proved the rule. The new Zachary Taylor administration was critical of Weller and sought to replace him with John Charles Frémont. Emory had testified against the Pathfinder at the Frémont court-martial and saw his potential appointment as a personal insult. As events fell out, Frémont declined the appointment, Emory was persuaded to continue with survey work, and Weller stayed on the job through the completion of the California survey. But experience on the San Diego-Gila River segment had been troubling. Topographical engineers resented Gray's high-handed ways and thought him incompetent. Separate appointments for commissioner and surveyor produced endless controversy. As Emory later explained, "A mixed commission, governed by persons wholly unused to public affairs, and ignorant of the first principles of the scientific knowledge involved in the questions to be determined by them" was a sure recipe for disaster.[4] And as Emory surely knew, the most complex and contentious portions of the survey were yet to come.

In early May 1850, with work not yet fully complete on the California survey, the Taylor administration appointed a new boundary commissioner. Few more extraordinary and miscast characters have marched through the pages of western exploration history than John Russell Bartlett. New York bookseller, bibliophile, and raconteur, Bartlett had all the right political and scientific connections but possessed neither leadership skills nor travel experience. His boundary commission, headed for a meeting with Mexican officials in El Paso, was a colorful but unwieldy collection of scientists, soldiers, civilian "mechanics," and a naval officer who served as Bartlett's personal publicity agent. Emory, one of Bartlett's sharpest critics, described the new commissioner's entourage as "a multitude of officers, quartermasters, commissaries, paymasters, agents, secretaries, sub-secretaries—all officers wholly unknown to any well-regulated surveying corps, and worse than useless by the conflict of authority which these officers engendered, and by the enormous expense which the payment of their salaries and personal expenses entailed on the commission."[5] Emory kept his distance from such a traveling sideshow; the army was ably represented by Lieutenant Colonel John McClellan as chief topographical engineer and Lieutenant Colonel James D. Graham as chief astronomer. Neither would have an easy time dealing with Bartlett.

After innumerable scrapes and endless escapades, Bartlett and an advance party reached
El Paso late in 1850. The Mexican commissioner was General Don Pedro García Conde,
an experienced army engineer and director of the *Colegio Militar*. Besides being an able
engineer, García Conde was also an astute diplomat. Bartlett was neither. After their first
meetings in December it was plain that the Disturnell maps and the treaty language simply
did not match astronomical observations and terrain realities. This was especially the case
for the location of New Mexico's southern boundary. The dispute was about much more
than land. Many Americans, including surveyor Gray and topographical engineers Amiel
W. Whipple and James D. Graham, believed that the territory claimed by García Conde to
be within Mexico was the best route for a southwestern railway to the Pacific. After endless
wrangling the two commissioners signed what came to be called the Bartlett-García Conde
Agreement (1851). Despite considerable protest—Gray had to be ordered by a cabinet
officer to sign the document—the compromise gave García Conde what he desired. And in
the meantime survey work moved slowly.

Dogged by controversy and incompetence from the beginning, the American boundary commission now seemed about to collapse. What the commission needed was an officer with scientific ability, considerable diplomatic skill, and good political connections in
Washington. Perhaps no one met those qualifications more fully than did William H.
Emory. By 1851 Emory was an experienced field surveyor with broad scientific interests
and a good sense for political reality. In September 1851 he was sent back into the boundary survey mess, this time as surveyor and chief astronomer. Late in the fall of 1851 Emory
reached El Paso and began a comprehensive reorganization of the American survey operation. Writing to his friend James A. Pearce, a Maryland politician, Emory explained: "I
have taken a different course from Colonel Graham; he stood still until he could get things
fixed to his liking. I have taken the means in hand and pressed the work to the utmost
[limits], indeed beyond them, and intend when a stop takes place to put the saddle on the
right horse."[6]

While Emory made significant progress by ignoring Bartlett, dealing with the Bartlett-
Conde Agreement proved much more difficult. After García Conde's unexpected death,
José Salazar Ylarregui was appointed acting Mexican commissioner. Salazar was a well-
trained professional engineer and, like Emory, an able diplomat. With Salazar unwilling to
change Mexico's position and considerable pressure coming from Washington, Emory was
in a difficult situation. Ordered by Secretary of the Interior Alexander Stuart to sign documents validating the compromise agreement, Emory knew that to do so would mean aban-
doning an important American claim. And it would surely mean the end of his military
career as well. Democrats in Congress were increasingly against the agreement. Emory's
personal view—one he made clear in correspondence in 1852 and later in his formal *Report*—was at odds with both Bartlett's supporters and his detractors. Based on his own
grasp of the southwestern terrain, Emory was convinced that the Bartlett-García Conde
line "was no worse [for a railway] than that claimed by his [Bartlett's] adversaries." Emory

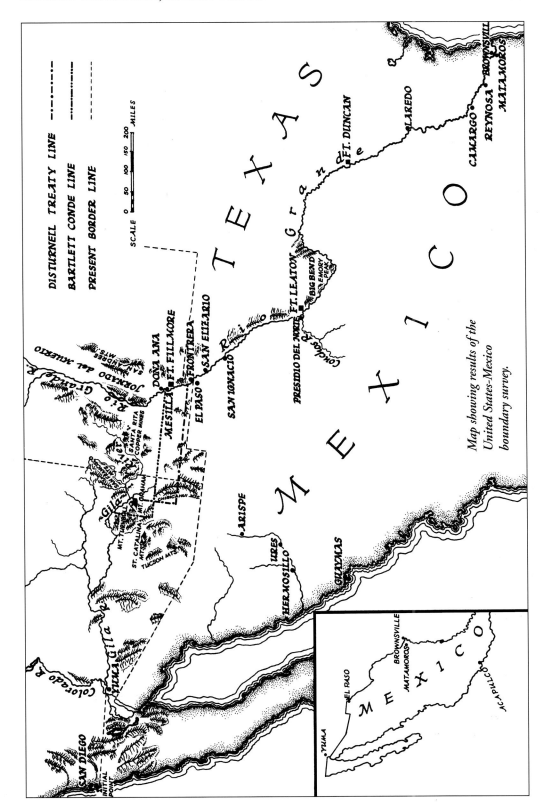

Map showing results of the
United States-Mexico
boundary survey.

and other topographical engineers believed that the best railway route was in fact consider-
ably to the south of "both of these lines of boundary."[7] Always an adept politician, Emory
escaped the trap when he met with Salazar in late August 1852. With considerable cun-
ning, Emory simply signed the Bartlett-García Conde Agreement maps as a witness to an
earlier agreement. As William H. Goetzmann explains, "By this expedient Stuart's order
had been obeyed, the Mexican commissioner was satisfied, the Democrats still had their
loophole, and his [Emory's] own career was saved."[8]

While Emory and Salazar were struggling over the thorny issues in a flawed agreement,
the United States Congress was again debating the future of the entire boundary survey.
Increasingly the debate was not about land for future settlement but how to secure the best
right-of-way for a future transcontinental railroad. The congressional debate raged for nearly
a year. Finally, in May 1853, General Robert B. Campbell was appointed as the new American
commissioner. It would be Campbell's responsibility to oversee completion of the survey of
the Rio Grande from the Gulf of Mexico to Laredo. But it was clearly understood that
Emory would have charge of all field operations. With his usual energy and organizational
skill, Emory and his team finished the river survey in September 1853.

Survey work was still far from complete. The Treaty of 1853, known in the United
States as the Gadsden Purchase and in Mexico as the Mesilla Treaty, had resolved prob-
lems with the original Treaty of 1848 and the recently rejected Bartlett-García Conde
Agreement. The 1853 treaty now required new surveys to link the California line to the
Rio Grande boundary. At long last American officials recognized that commissions
with joint civilian and military leadership simply did not work. In mid August 1854
Emory was appointed chief astronomer and commissioner for what proved to be the
last of the boundary commissions. Because Emory and Salazar maintained a close personal and professional relationship, survey work moved quickly during 1855. Considerable credit for the speed and efficiency of that work belonged to two topographical
engineers: Lieutenant Nathaniel Michler and Lieutenant William Turnbull. By mid
October 1855 field work was complete. Preparation of finished maps and an official
report remained.

Emory once complained that writing a history of the boundary survey commissions
"would no doubt be instructive," but the story was so filled with controversy and acrimony
"as to make the task both complicated and unpleasant."[9] While the story in the field and in
the halls of Congress was contentious, the report prepared by Emory and his group of
scientists proved remarkably valuable. William H. Goetzmann writes that the Emory report "is a monumental contribution to American geography." What Emory produced,
Goetzmann observes, was "nineteenth-century state-of-the-art geography."[10] Published in
three well-illustrated volumes between 1857 and 1859, the *Report of the United States and
Mexican Boundary Survey* combined Emory's cartographic and topographical studies with
evaluations of regional plants and animals. But unlike other contemporary exploration
accounts, Emory paid little attention to ethnography. In his overview of the survey he

explained that "I have said nothing in this sketch of the races of man which inhabit this vast western region." Those observations were to be included in "the more detailed description of each portion of the boundary line."[11]

By the 1850s geographically minded explorers like Emory were struggling to reconceptualize the physical landscape of North America. The simplicities in Jefferson's vision that informed the Lewis and Clark journey were rapidly dissolving into a far more complex, scientific understanding of climate and landform. While the approach taken by Alexander von Humboldt (1769-1859) is often linked to that growing continental vision, Emory was strikingly critical of the German geographer. Humboldt's grand scheme, embraced by many geographers and explorers, sought to discover "the higher laws of nature, which govern the universe, men, animals, plants, and minerals."[12] Ridiculing what he called "hypothetical geography," Emory insisted that "this pernicious system was commenced under the eminent auspices of Baron Humboldt, who, from a few excursions into Mexico, attempted to figure out the whole North American continent."[13] Reflecting the cautious, observation-by-observation approach he shared with Abert, Emory avoided making grand, sweeping generalizations about a complex western landscape.

Based on his own extensive experience, Emory was ready to make at least one sweeping statement about the character of the West beyond the 100th meridian. Troubled by what he called "fanciful and exaggerated" descriptions of the West advanced by promoters and entrepreneurs, Emory felt bound to offer a more realistic description of the region he knew so well. Writing some two decades before John Wesley Powell's famous *Report on the Lands of the Arid Region of the United States* (1879), Emory insisted that "whatever may be said to the contrary, these plains west of the 100th meridian are wholly unsusceptible of sustaining an agricultural population." Despite enduring visions of the West as the Garden of the World, Emory maintained that aridity was the fundamental western fact of life. The farming practices that were so successful in the East were unsuited for western realities.

Again well ahead of his time, Emory concluded:

Whatever population may now, or hereafter, occupy the mountain system, and the plains to the east, must be dependent on mining, or grazing, or the cultivation of the grape. The country must be settled by a mining and pastoral or wine-making population; and the whole legislation of Congress, directed heretofore so successfully towards the settlement of lands east of the 100th meridian of longitude, must be remodeled and reorganized to suit the new phase which life must assume under conditions so different from those to which we are accustomed.[14]

Historians are fond of naming certain periods in history as the Age of ——— or the Era of ———. So we have the Age of Jackson or the Era of Reconstruction. In many ways much of the nineteenth century, both in Europe and America, was the Age of the Iron Horse. No single invention more profoundly shaped both daily life and national ambitions than the railroad. The steam locomotive came to represent all that was vital and dynamic in modern life. For many, the railroad depot seemed the gatehouse to a bright future. Time and distance were transformed. As Asa Whitney, intellectual godfather and tireless promoter of the Pacific railroad put it, "time and space are annihilated by steam."[15] Perhaps no one more fully captured the sense of wonder and possibility that railroads offered than did Ralph Waldo Emerson. Writing in 1844, the same year that Whitney formulated his pioneer transcontinental proposal, Emerson exclaimed, "Railroad iron is a magician's rod, in its power to evoke the sleeping energies of land and water."[16]

Asa Whitney, sometime merchant in the China trade and full-time railway visionary, was not the first to suggest building a railroad across the continent to the Pacific. But no one else had Whitney's energy and imagination, and few could match his dogged determination. In late January 1845, after months of thinking and planning, Whitney sent to Congress his proposal "to construct a railroad from Lake Michigan to the Pacific Ocean." Short on route information and construction details, Whitney's plan made grand promises: A Pacific railroad "will produce commercial, political, and national results and benefits, which must be seen and felt throughout our vast confederacy."[17] But in July 1846 the House Committee on Roads and Canals was not persuaded, finding Whitney's scheme "too gigantic, and, at least for the present, entirely impracticable."[18] Thomas Hart Benton, so often considered a champion of expansion, mocked Whitney's ideas as a "humbug" that "emanated only from a madman."[19]

But what seemed preposterous and impractical in 1846 became by 1849 a national passion embraced by scores of cities and dozens of national politicians. Whitney's "humbug" now seemed almost a settled fact of American life. In those few short years so much had changed. Territorial acquisitions stemming from the Mexican War made the United States a continental nation. From a military standpoint there were new territories to defend, with questions about unknown terrain and long supply lines. Hard on the heels of war's end came the discovery of gold in California. Explorations by Frémont and Emory suggested that there were possible railway routes across the continent. Emory's 1846 report was especially important, noting the 32d parallel-Gila River route to California. And in all of this there was the ceaseless lobbying done by Whitney and others. The Mexican War and California gold had changed the geopolitical shape of North America. In three years' time a railway project that had once seemed impossible now appeared as one more sign of America's imperial future.

By the end of the Mexican War talk about a Pacific railroad was everywhere. Newspapers, pamphlets, petitions to Congress, and local meetings all demanded that work begin immediately on a transcontinental line. The arguments for such a railroad centered on three important questions. The first of those was national development. Senator Benton, now converted to the railroad gospel, echoed Emerson by declaring: "An American road to India through the heart of our country will revive upon its line all the wonders of which we have read—and eclipse them. The western wilderness, from the Pacific to the

Mississippi, will start into life under its touch."[20] While not so lyrical, *American Railway Journal* editor Henry Varnum Poor was no less direct. Western railways "will not only in many cases double the value [of land], but it will infinitely increase the amount of agricultural production."[21]

Others saw the transcontinental railroad in terms of national unity. At a time of growing sectional rivalry—with debates that would eventually lead to the Compromise of 1850—many argued that a Pacific railroad would link the nation and preserve the Union. As the editor of the Trenton, Tennessee, *Emporium* put it, "These railroads are the iron bands that will bind the various sections of our beloved country together by a community of interest and fraternal feeling, and it is hoped, will render our Union indissoluable."[22] To the arguments about economic growth and national unity were added images of imperial greatness. A transcontinental railroad would be a sure sign of America's continental power. As one congressman grandly put it, the Pacific railroad was "necessary to the highest destiny of the nation."[23] The American empire would have two emblems—the flag and the locomotive.

As the chorus of voices calling for a Pacific railway swelled, two things became increasingly clear. First, Congress was going to authorize only one line across the country. From that political and financial reality flowed a second, unpleasant fact. A dozen cities now advanced themselves as the ideal eastern terminal. This rivalry has often been described in sectional terms, presaging the coming conflict between North and South. But the political controversy about routes and terminals was more complex. The debate was as much within sections as between them. From St. Paul and Chicago to St. Louis, Memphis, and Vicksburg, cities held railroad conventions, drafted congressional proposals, and sent spokesmen to Washington. The Senate and House chambers rang with speeches detailing the perfection of St. Louis's central route or the ideal passage to the orient from Memphis. Each city claimed pride of place, thinking it would win a bonanza in the riches of the "Great West." By 1853 Congress was hopelessly deadlocked. No single Pacific railway proposal had enough support to win approval and some were beginning to doubt if the government would ever authorize so important a national project.

Route selection, once an engineering question, had become a political nightmare. Perhaps the way out of that bad dream was to settle the question by the cold light of Reason and Science. There was nothing new in the notion that science could play a key role in public policy. Banks and Jefferson had subscribed to such a view, and by the 1850s faith in the objective power of science was growing. For two senators—William Gwin of California and Richard Brodhead of Pennsylvania—science did seem the answer to the railroad impasse. Their proposal was simple: Congress would direct Secretary of War Jefferson Davis to order survey teams from the Corps of Topographical Engineers into the field. Using the best equipment available, soldier-explorers would examine the routes and determine which one was "the most practicable and economical."[24] Gwin and Brodhead thought that the entire exploration and evaluation process could be accomplished in ten months, giving Congress its desired answer in January 1854. The Pacific Railroad Survey bill was passed on

March 2, 1853, and, trusting in science and the soldier-explorers, Congress waited to be rescued from the railway mess.

But the soldier-explorers—and the legislation that sent them marching over western rights-of-way—were not without their critics. No one was more strident in his criticism than Senator Benton. Benton had once strongly supported the army's role in western exploration, but the bitterness over the Frémont court-martial had soured that relationship. The senator was persuaded that Secretary Davis, Colonel Abert, and Major Emory had conspired to prejudice the entire survey in favor of the 32d parallel route. Benton aggressively supported a central route from St. Louis. It was common knowledge, so he charged, that Davis and the army had already decided for personal and political reasons to support a more southern line. Benton was especially suspicious of Emory. The major had testified against Frémont, he had supported the 32d parallel route for several years, and Benton insinuated that Emory personally stood to gain by having the railway built through the Southwest. Emory's brother-in-law was Robert J. Walker, president of the Atlantic and Pacific Railroad Company. That company was intent on building a line to the Pacific roughly along the route Emory had long favored. However, as William H. Goetzmann's careful research has shown, there is no evidence that Emory had any financial arrangement with Walker. But in the broadest sense, Benton was right. Davis, Abert, and Emory were predisposed to favor a more southern route. As Davis explained some years later, when no longer Secretary of War, "If the section of which I am a citizen has the best route, I ask who that looks to the interest of the country has a right to deny it the road?"[25]

Sensitive to the criticism leveled by Benton and others, Davis, Abert, and Emory were careful in their selection of officers to lead the various surveys. Perhaps confident that science would validate their southern route, they saw no reason to "fix" the survey leadership. What the army now faced was its most demanding exploration mission. Expedition teams had to be organized and outfitted, route decisions had to be made, and an entire command structure within the corps had to be established. All of this—from Washington office to field work to finished report—had to be accomplished in less than a year. Moving quickly, Davis and his officers established the Bureau of Western Explorations and Surveys—a separate unit within the Corps of Topographical Engineers and under the direction of Emory and Captain Andrew A. Humphreys. That bureau would oversee the entire railroad survey enterprise, keeping track of everything from personnel applications and field records to requisitions for scientific instruments and camp supplies.

Early in the planning process several key decisions shaped the course of the railway surveys. Emory's unhappy experience with the mixed civilian-military leadership in the Mexican Boundary Survey made it plain that the Pacific Railway Survey parties were to be under military control. Initially there were to be four survey expeditions tracing routes along four distinct East-West corridors. Two additional ones were added later. Perhaps

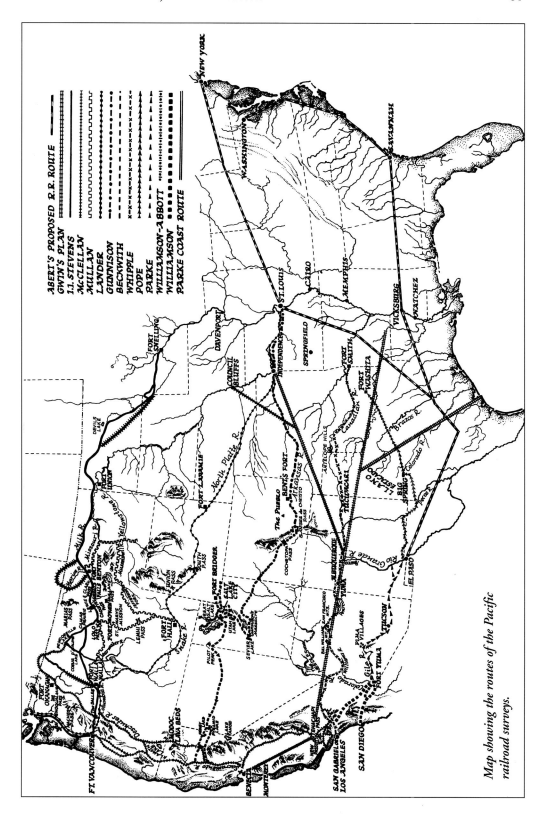

Map showing the routes of the Pacific railroad surveys.

most consequential decision came as officers like Abert and Emory began to consider the scope and range of the surveys themselves. Congress expected a simple answer, something that could be summed up in a short engineering report. But the soldier-explorers and their scientist colleagues understood the surveys in a very different way. They envisioned the expeditions as grand intellectual ventures, an opportunity to study the entire American continent. They planned on exploring not just lines but entire regional corridors. In this way the railway expeditions pointed toward the post-Civil War territorial surveys. Perhaps now the detailed instructions Jefferson gave Lewis could finally be fulfilled as the soldier-explorers and their scientist friends made plain "the face of the country."

William H. Goetzmann once described the railroad survey expedition led by Isaac I. Stevens as "the first and the most elaborate to take to the field."[26] An army engineer with experience in coastal survey work, Stevens had resigned his commission to become governor of Washington Territory. A tireless promoter of the region, Stevens was known to all as a man of great energy and wide-ranging imagination. And it was hardly a secret that Stevens linked his own political future to a railroad route favoring the Pacific Northwest. Of all the survey commanders, no one proved more an advocate for the route he surveyed than Stevens.

On at least one thing Stevens and the army leadership agreed. The expeditions were to gather more than just engineering information. Stevens wrote his own exploration instructions and whether he knew it or not his document was as broad as the one Jefferson prepared for Lewis. Stevens sent his soldier-explorers "to examine carefully the passes of the several mountain ranges, the geography and meteorology of the whole intermediate region, the character, as avenues of trade and transportation, of the Missouri and Columbia rivers, the rains and snows of the route, especially the mountain passes, and in short, to collect every species of information bearing upon the question of railroad practibility." Stevens also hoped "to give great attention to the Indian tribes, as their friendship [is] important to be secured, and [bears] directly upon the question of the Pacific railroad and the safety of my party."[27]

In order to accomplish these ambitious goals, Stevens divided his large expedition into two parties. The main body, personally led by Stevens, would head west from St. Paul. The western unit, commanded by Captain George B. McClellan out of Vancouver Barracks, was directed to locate and survey appropriate passes in the Cascade range. Stevens recruited a large contingent of regular army officers and civilian scientists, including geologists, naturalists, and ethnographers. And for the visual record there were artists John Mix Stanley and Gustav Sohon. Grasping the significance of the survey journey, Stanley went so far as to draft a brief but important "Memorandum in Relation to Sketches in Natural History, Geology, Botany and to Views of Scenery and Natural Objects" that would guide his artistic work. "Sketches of Indians," wrote Stanley, "should be made and colored from life, with care to fidelity to complexion as well as feature." Stanley was also interested in geological and landform illustration, noting that "sketches of geological formulations, rock exposures etc. may frequently be made to great advantage."[28]

The main Stevens survey expedition took to the field in early June 1853. Sounding much like Lewis and Clark, Stevens sought routes and passes that would connect the Missouri River to the Columbia. If waterways could not provide the long sought-after Northwest Passage, perhaps railways would be the modern "passage to India." At the same time, McClellan's expedition struggled through demanding country to find and evaluate Cascades passes. As fortune had it, McClellan failed to measure snow depths at Snoqualmie Pass, the one route that might have proved practical for a northern rail line.

Despite all the problems that a northern route presented—everything from snow to expensive tunnels and grades—Stevens prepared an optimistic report. He dismissed the snow question, claiming that according to "the accounts of all who have traversed the Rocky mountains during almost every winter month, the snow there met with would not present the slightest impediment to the constant passage of railroad trains."[29] Having brushed aside blizzards and avalanches, Stevens dismissed claims that the land along the route could never sustain agricultural settlement. Based on more faith than evidence, he asserted that the country along the northern route "compares favorably with the best portions of the empire of Russia for cultivation of the great staples of agriculture, and west of the Rocky mountains far surpasses them, approaching the most productive countries of Europe."[30] Blessed with "a milder climate than Wisconsin or Iowa, or any part of Nebraska east of the 100th meridian," Stevens's northern West contained "nothing in the soil of any portion, except the western part of the Columbia, which forbids agriculture."[31]

If Stevens convinced himself that his northern railroad was both practical and economical he found few converts in the Bureau of Western Explorations and Surveys. While the finished survey reports were still in the making, Captain Humphreys and Lieutenant Gouverneur Kemble Warren prepared a preliminary set of findings. Published in early 1855, the Humphreys-Warren report made it clear that the War Department would not support Stevens's recommendations. Humphreys and Warren acknowledged that the governor's findings were "forcibly and clearly written" and then proceeded to demolish most of the explorer's arguments.[32] The topographical engineers disputed Stevens's construction cost and time estimates, insisting that those figures "cannot be founded upon the experience of any great line of railroad built in the United States."[33] The bureau calculated that Stevens's costs would have to be expanded by 100 percent even to begin to match reality. But Humphreys and Warren saved their harshest criticism for Stevens's vision of the northern country as the Jeffersonian Garden of the World. Why, asked the army officers, should Congress build the only transcontinental line through so desolate a country? Of the proposed 2,025 miles of line between St. Paul and Seattle, "we have only a space of about 535 miles of fertile country; the remaining 1,490 miles being over uncultivable prairie soil, or mountain-land producing only timber, with the limited exception of occasional river bottoms, mountain valleys, or prairie."[34] But Humphreys and Warren were not the only

"Herd of Bison, near Lake Jessie, North Dakota," by John Mix Stanley for the Pacific railroad report of the Stevens survey.

skeptics. Expedition naturalist George Suckley ridiculed Stevens's schemes, writing that "a road *might* be built over the tops of the Himalayeh mountains—but no reasonable man would undertake it. I think the same of the Northern route."[35]

Having eliminated Stevens's survey from the route competition, Humphreys and Warren proceeded to evaluate the other expedition reports now coming in to their Washington headquarters. The route following the 41st and 42d parallels from the Missouri River along the Platte and over South Pass did not, so the army believed, warrant a full field survey. Drawing on the previous Frémont and Howard Stansbury expeditions, with additional work done by Lieutenant Edward G. Beckwith, Humphreys and Warren found that while the route was possible it would probably prove difficult and expensive. The central route (38th to 39th parallels), so long advocated by Benton and the St. Louis interests, had been ably explored by Lieutenant John W. Gunnison. But the deaths of Gunnison and several of his party at the hands of Indians in late October 1853 had cut that survey short. Work was partially completed by Lieutenant Beckwith. Treading carefully on what they knew was a popular route with strong congressional support, Humphreys and Warren played a "now you see it, now you don't" game. Reporting on the route from the Rockies to the Great Basin, the bureau declared that this portion "would probably give the shortest road from the Bay of San Francisco to the navigable waters of the Mississippi." But in evaluating the entire central route the story was very different. "The country is so broken," claimed Humphreys and Warren, "and the difficulties of construction so great, and the expense would be so enormous, that the building of a railroad over this portion may be pronounced as impracticable."[36]

Like Secretary Davis and others in the Corps of Topographical Engineers establishment, Humphreys and Warren favored a more southern route. Yet the survey along the 35th parallel conducted by Lieutenant Amiel W. Whipple mapped a route that seemed practical and enjoyed substantial popular support. While not giving it pride of place, Humphreys and Warren did recognize the obvious advantages in such a right-of-way. It could serve a number of eastern terminals, thereby satisfying several regional constituencies. Construction materials were readily available, locomotive fuel supplies were generally reliable, and the grades were comparable to those on the widely recognized benchmark Baltimore and Ohio Railroad. But it came as no surprise that the great bulk of the Humphreys-Warren report was devoted to the 32d parallel route. Drawing on a whole generation of soldier-explorer work, and supplemented with a recent survey conducted by Captain John Pope, Humphreys and Warren drafted what amounted to a promotional pamphlet for the 32d parallel line. For these officers the advantages of the Gila River passage seemed obvious: "low elevation of the mountain passes"; "favorable topographical features" all along the line; "temperate climate"; and the "shortness of the line"—a mere 1,600 miles from the Mississippi to the Pacific.[37] But no engineering feature was more important, so Humphreys and Warren argued, as the matter of the right-of-way itself. Other routes had to challenge formidable mountain barriers. "The great advantage of this route is, that for the space of 1,100 or 1,200 miles, the usual item of great expense in railroads is in great measure avoided, there being no necessity to prepare an expensive roadbed except in a few instances in the passage of the mountain chains."[38]

At the end of February 1855 Secretary Davis announced his official recommendation for a transcontinental railway route. Anyone who had paid the slightest attention to the Humphreys-Warren report was not surprised by what the secretary said. His support for the southern, 32d parallel route was blunt and unequivocal. Careful study of the topographical engineers' surveys "conclusively shows that the route of the 32d parallel is, of those surveyed, 'the most practicable and economical route for a railroad from the Mississippi River to the Pacific Ocean.'"[39] Davis argued that climate, terrain, cost, and distance all favored the southern route. The conclusion seemed obvious to him: "not only is this the shortest and least costly route to the Pacific, but it is the shortest and cheapest route to San Francisco, the greatest commercial city on our western coast."[40]

Davis and the soldier-explorers may have found their arguments compelling; many in Congress did not. As William H. Goetzmann observes, a careful reading of the survey reports makes it plain that there were several practical and economical lines to the Pacific. Davis's critics found it easy to charge the secretary and his officers with sectional bias. And Davis added fuel to that fire by comments he made years later while senator from Mississippi, indirectly linking his decision to state and regional loyalties. But as Goetzmann explains, Davis's motives were more complex than simple sectional bias. From the time of the Mexican War soldier-explorers had focused much personal and professional energy on the geographic exploration of the Southwest. Emory was not the only topographical engineer to have an entire exploration career invested in the region. What Davis inherited as secretary of war, and fully embraced, was an institutional mindset fixed on the Southwest. In a very real sense the soldier-explorers suffered from a kind of self-fulfilling prophecy that tended to exaggerate certain regional advantages while turning a blind eye to the possibilities afforded by other areas. What seemed obvious to Davis, Abert, Emory, and Humphreys appeared far less so to members of Congress and their constituents. The War Department insisted that evidence supported only one route; others who read the same reports came to very different conclusions. Politics, personal experience, and institutional tradition led the soldier-explorers into a box canyon. Despite their best intentions they failed in their mission. Few in Congress now thought that the soldier-explorers could resolve the railroad tangle. That resolution—the route taken by the Union Pacific and the Central Pacific—came only after southern delegations left Congress in 1861. War and civilian railroad surveyors decided what the soldier-explorers could not.

At the simplest level the Pacific Railroad Surveys were an expensive failure, one that embarrassed the War Department and damaged the reputation of the Corps of Topographical Engineers. But anyone paging through the twelve massive, lavishly illustrated volumes of the *Reports of Explorations and Surveys, to ascertain the most practicable and economical route for a railroad from the Mississippi River to the Pacific Ocean* will surely come to a different conclusion. Goetzmann has aptly described the survey volumes as "an American encyclopedia of western experience."[41] Congress expected that science would serve the public interest and resolve a contentious national question. As fortune had it, it was Congress and the federal treasury that served science and the empire of the mind. Early in the planning of the surveys, Davis and his advisors envisioned the field expeditions as far more than engineering reconnaissances. Making good on their long-term relationship with leading American scientists, the soldier-explorers began to recruit scientifically minded personnel for the survey parties. The Bureau of Western Explorations and Surveys especially relied on advice and recommendations from four distinguished scholars: Spencer F. Baird, assistant secretary at the Smithsonian Institution; geologist James Hall, the influential botanist John Torrey; and Harvard University naturalist and zoologist Louis Agassiz. These men represented a powerful scientific lobby, setting research agendas and working to secure appointments on survey expeditions for students and colleagues. For the first time, and almost in spite of itself, the federal government became a patron for what was later called "Big Science."

For the modern reader nothing is more compelling in those hefty survey volumes than the landscape drawings and scientific illustrations. This was the West visualized in sweeping prairie vistas, towering mountain views, and panoramic scenes of imperial grandeur. This was the West personalized in remarkable portraits of native inhabitants. And this was the West revealed in vivid, colorful drawings of exotic plants, remarkable animals, and fossils from an ancient America. The railroad surveys attracted some of the period's most talented artists and illustrators, including John Mix Stanley, Richard H.

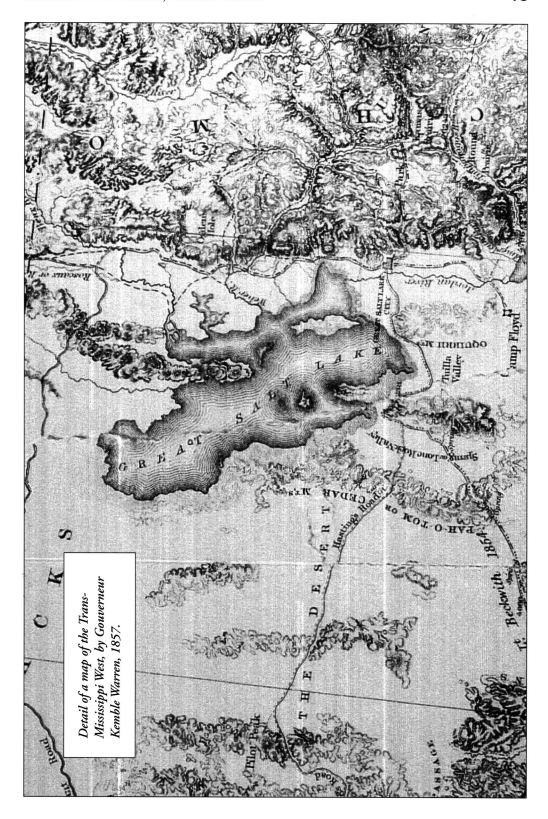

Detail of a map of the Trans-Mississippi West, by Gouverneur Kemble Warren, 1857.

Kern, Gustav Sohon, Baron F. W. Egloffstein, and Heinrich B. Mollhausen. All told, expedition artists produced 147 lithographs. In addition, there were countless scientific illustrations, all making what had seemed an empty country suddenly full of life. And buried in volume eleven of the reports was the survey's greatest cartographic achievement. Working from his bureau office in Washington, Lieutenant Warren began a comprehensive study of the available cartographic materials for the entire West. What Warren produced—in a map nearly three feet by four feet—was a remarkable vision of the West as a complex region filled with mountain ranges, river systems, desert countries, and prairie lands. What had begun with William Clark's master map of 1810 and the printed version in 1814 was now nearly complete in Warren's remarkable synthesis. Warren, and the draftsmen who worked for him, crafted a map of imperial size for a nation of imperial ambitions. Perhaps more than any other single item, the Warren map of 1857 represented the accomplishments of the soldier-explorers.

Throughout the 1840s and 1850s the Corps of Topographical Engineers enjoyed unparalleled influence as the nation's premier explorers of the West. Despite criticism about the corps' role in the railroad surveys, Abert and his officers continued their grand reconnaissance of the West. No one better represented that stalwart, reliable service than Captain James H. Simpson. West Point Class of 1832, Simpson joined the Corps of Topographical Engineers as one of its original officers in 1838. His first western tour came with Captain Randolph Marcy's expedition through the Texas-Oklahoma border country in 1849. Simpson spent 1851-56 surveying wagon roads in Minnesota before returning to the West to conduct a grand sweep in the Great Basin in 1858-59. Devoted to the army's wagon road program, Simpson was not drawn into the railroad frenzy, nor did he write inflated reports about Edens in the Southwest. From Minnesota to Utah by way of Texas and New Mexico, Simpson saw more of the West in ten years than any other soldier-explorer.

But in so many ways time was not on the side of Abert's explorers. An aging Colonel Abert retired in 1861, the same year that the Civil War drew topographical engineers away from the West and into bloody fields of fire. While most topographical engineers remained in the United States Army, nine officers exchanged blue uniforms for gray ones. On whatever side they fought, the soldier-explorers proved exceptional soldiers. Emory once again earned his nickname, "Bold Emory," as a superb Union cavalry commander; Joseph Christmas Ives—explorer of the Grand Canyon of the Colorado—became personal aide to Confederate President Jefferson Davis, and Amiel W. Whipple was killed at the Battle of Chancellorsville. But no former soldier-explorer played so dramatic a role at a decisive moment in the war as did G. K. Warren at Gettysburg. As chief engineer to former Topographical Engineer General George G. Meade, Warren quickly understood the significance of Little Round Top for the command of the entire field. With a handful of men Warren took the hill and began the battle for Gettysburg's most strategic place.

Warren and his fellow officers were part of saving the Union, but they could not save the Corps of Topographical Engineers. With Abert gone and the corps scattered, it was plain that the unit's days as a separate outfit were numbered. In March 1863 the Corps of Topographical Engineers ceased to exist, its personnel now part of the larger Corps of Engineers. But the army's exploration mission—begun with Jefferson and advanced by Abert—was not about to slip away so quickly. After the Civil War, soldier-explorers would again look West, perhaps hoping to recover faded glory.

Chapter

ARMY EXPLORERS AND THE GREAT WEST

Perhaps no one more fully grasped the enormous changes the Civil War made in American life better than Mark Twain. In his prophetic, satirical novel, *The Gilded Age* (1873), coauthored with Samuel Dudley Warner, Twain wrote: "The eight years in America from 1860 to 1868 uprooted institutions that were centuries old, changed the politics of a people, transformed the social life of half the country, and wrought so profoundly upon the entire national character that the influence cannot be measured short of two or three generations."[1]

After the war there was a reorientation of national energies. In the first half of the nineteenth century national politics had run along North and South lines, following sectional disputes about race and slavery. The West figured in those debates only in terms of arguments about the extension of slavery. When the nation did face west it was to the edges of the continent, to Pacific shores and the Southwest. After the war it was the economic potential of Great Plains and the interior West that captured national attention. That West was seen in terms of natural resources for an industrial East. Land for farms, cows instead of bison, and minerals of all sorts were part of what journalists and travelers called "The Great West." The development ideas so common in the Pacific railway debates surfaced once again as the interior West was portrayed as the nation's treasure chest. Colonel Sellers, Twain's archetypical promoter in *The Gilded Age*, put it best. "The whole country is opening up, all we want is capital to develop it. Slap down the rails and bring the land into market. The richest land on God Almighty's footstool is lying right out there."[2]

Soldier-explorers had once sketched the outlines of Jefferson's western garden. Now what an industrial nation demanded was an accounting of what lay beneath the surface of "the face of the country." Scientific surveys would enable farmers, ranchers, mining engineers, and railway builders to make good on the promise of what Hartford, Connecticut, newspaperman and western traveler Samuel Bowles called "Our New West."

No soldier-explorer could have marched his way west without the orders, guidance, and support of well-placed patrons. President Thomas Jefferson, Secretaries of War John C.

Calhoun and Jefferson Davis, and Colonel John J. Abert drafted those orders and provided that patronage. But after the Civil War, with the disappearance of the Corps of Topographical Engineers, some might have wondered who would supply the energy and influence to keep the army in the exploration game. That direction came from the army's chief of engineers, General Andrew A. Humphreys. In many ways, Humphreys was Abert's logical successor. West Point Class of 1831 and one of the original Corps of Topographical Engineers officers, Humphreys ran the Bureau of Western Explorations and Surveys, had a distinguished Civil War combat record, and possessed a comprehensive understanding of the army's post-Civil War role in the West. From 1866 through the end of the 1870s Humphreys used all his bureaucratic skill and political influence to keep the army in the forefront of scientific exploration.

Clarence King was the first of two major post-Civil War explorers to enjoy Humphreys' support. Born into a Newport, Rhode Island, merchant family, King entered Yale University in 1860. Instead of following the usual classical course of study, King became a student at the Sheffield Scientific School, taking courses in geology and chemistry. Yale was King's intellectual foundation, but the real building of his western scientific career began when he went west to join Josiah Dwight Whitney's California Geological Survey. Those who knew him in California could not escape noting his restless energy, powerful ambition, and keen, analytical intellect. Distinguished writer and historian Henry Adams, who knew King well, insisted that the world had only one Clarence King.

In 1866, while on an exploring expedition with James T. Gardner, King looked out over the Great Basin and gave final shape to what would become his grand survey plan. That plan involved studying large geographic areas, not searching for routes to the Pacific or marking international boundaries. Later that year King went to Washington and presented his 40th parallel survey idea to Secretary of War Edwin Stanton. King brought the War Department not only a fully developed exploration plan but also the connections—personal and professional—that he had with leading academic scientists. And like William H. Emory, King was as much at home in the corridors of social and political power as in the most rugged western terrain. In 1867 King obtained a two-year appropriation from the War Department for his expedition. Then, working in conjunction with General Humphreys, King began to fashion a remarkable exploring party. While the army would provide an escort of tough troopers from the Eighth Cavalry, King's principal assistants were all civilians. Who he selected for the survey reveals something about the growing professionalization and specialization of knowledge. Gone were the days of the all-around naturalist. In his place came highly trained geologists like Samuel F. Emmons and the brothers Arnold and James D. Hague. King's principal topographer was James T. Gardner, his colleague and friend from California days. Botany came under the purview of William Whitman Bailey, Jr.; young Robert Ridgway was expedition ornithologist. As Martha A. Sandweiss writes in her definitive history of western photography, "photographers would be an essential part of the survey crews."[3] King recruited Civil War photographer Timothy

"Clarence King in camp at Salt Lake City," photo by O'Sullivan, 1868-69.

O'Sullivan to capture visual images of the landscape. As a sign of changing times, King did not take along an ethnographer. What mattered was the wealth of the land; native inhabitants were, so he believed, either a curiosity or an irritation. Sergeant Edward Schwartz's cavalrymen would take care of Indians. Henry Adams, who visited the King survey in 1871, caught something of the spirit of those explorers. "They held under their hammers a thousand miles of mineral country with all its riddles to solve, and its stores of possible wealth to mark."[4]

Like Isaac Stevens, King wrote his own instructions. The document plainly reflected the powerful economic forces that informed his entire survey. Prepared in March 1867, the instructions were vast in their geographic range.

> *The object of the exploration is to examine and describe the geological structure, geographical condition and natural resources of a belt of country extending from the 120th meridian eastward to the 105th meridian, along the 40th parallel of latitude with significant expansion north and south to include the line of the "Central" and "Union Pacific" railroads and as much more as may be consistent with accuracy and proper progress.*[5]

King hoped to link his survey with the California Geological Survey and complete the entire enterprise in two years. In his first published report (1878) King put his strategy into even sharper focus. "The Exploration of the Fortieth Parallel promised, first, a study and description of all the natural resources of the mountain country near the Union and Central Pacific railroads; secondly, the completion of a continuous geological section across the widest expansion of the Great Cordilleran Mountain System."[6]

What lay behind King's instructions was a vision of the West and the nation shared by both army officers and civilian politicians and entrepreneurs. In an expanding industrial economy the West would be the mineral treasure house, providing gold, silver, coal, and other ores. And railroads would bring mineral wealth out of the West and settlers into the region. All this economic development could in a short time simply overwhelm the native nations, making further resistance impossible. Such a plan fit neatly with the military approaches envisioned by General William T. Sherman. King was no soldier, but his explorations became part of the army's larger strategy to make the West safe for cows, corn, and capital.

King and his party began their work in the summer of 1867 by exploring and mapping the desert and mountain country of western Nevada. During that first summer King made clear the exploration plan he would follow in the years to come. "This work," he wrote, "is not a geological survey, but a rapid exploration of a very great area, in which literally nothing but a few isolated details were before known. Unmapped, unstudied, it was terra incognita."[7] Struggling through difficult country and suffering from malaria, King's "ardent and

"King survey wagon on the sand dunes, Carson Desert, Great Basin,"
photo by Timothy O'Sullivan, 1867.

untiring corps" barely made it into winter camp.[8] During the winter of 1867-68 King undertook a comprehensive study of the mines at the Comstock Lode. Geologist James D. Hague later made a similar study of the gold and silver mines in Colorado. During the second exploration season King extended his work across the Great Basin as far as the Great Salt Lake. Having now run out of time and money, the explorer returned to Washington, played a masterful political game, and secured additional funding at a time when—in William H. Goetzmann's words—Congress "was feeling bearish on the subject of government surveys."[9]

Back in the field once again, King and his explorers made major discoveries—most notably they were the first to scientifically describe an active glacier in the United States, in the Shasta country. But King was always more than a scientific explorer on the army payroll. What he also enjoyed was literary fame and the pleasures of high society. His adventures, and a friendship with California writer Bret Harte, soon made King a celebrity. Encouraged by Harte and publisher James T. Fields, King wrote a series of articles about his western exploits for the prestigious *Atlantic Monthly*. Encouraged by this success, King decided to put his stories into a book. *Mountaineering in the Sierra Nevada* (1872) was a triumph for King, making him a national figure and further expanding a romantic vision of the West.

By 1872 King was plainly weary of exploration's constant travel demands. General Humphreys wanted to keep the King survey in the field and King needed the general's support. That year—1872—proved to be King's grandest, the year he entered western mythology. Early that year two prospectors arrived in San Francisco claiming to have found a fabulous diamond mine. News spread quickly and when New York jeweler Charles Tiffany declared that the samples were authentic and worth "a rajah's ransom," investors were ready to act. Reflecting the expansive rhetoric of the age, the New York and San Francisco Mining and Commercial Company seemed ready to make fortunes for plungers on both coasts.

Because the diamond field supposedly lay in country they had explored, King and other members of the survey were both fascinated and perplexed by the purported discovery. In October 1872 King and several others found the supposed diamond site and soon discovered that it had been salted. King rushed back to San Francisco, confronted the horrified company directors, and exposed the hoax. Overnight King became a hero. Science had saved the stockholders; geology was more than an idle academic pursuit.

By the end of 1873 King's years in the field were over. But what he had accomplished was nothing short of astounding. William H. Goetzmann notes, "As a great and epic feat of exploration and adventure, the King Survey surpassed everything else that had been done in the latter-day West except perhaps Major Powell's dramatic descent of the Grand Canyon."[10] Always something of a self-promoter, King understood the magnitude—or at least the geographic scope—of his enterprise. Writing in 1878, he said: "It has fallen to the lot of one set of observers to become intimate with so wide a range of horizons and products."[11] King plainly enjoyed his role as a romantic adventurer, but he never abandoned the notion that science had practical applications. Once describing his work as "a stepping-stone worthy to be built into the great stairway of science," King measured knowledge by its utility.[12] Like Jefferson, King believed that knowledge unpublished was knowledge lost. Writing to General Humphreys in 1874, King argued that "the day has passed in geological science when it is either decent or tolerable to rush into print with undigested operations, ignoring the methods and appliances in use among advanced investigators." King hoped to give his published survey reports "a finish which will place it on an equal footing with the best European publications."[13]

The seven heavily illustrated volumes of the *Report of the Geological Exploration of the Fortieth Parallel*, published between 1878 and 1880, represented the very best in American scientific exploration. While King's *Systematic Geology* (1878) is often pointed to as the survey's most compelling book, readers with an eye to future western economic development were probably more attracted to James D. Hague's *Mining Industry* (1879). Based on extensive field work in present-day Nevada, Utah, and Colorado, this volume offered a comprehensive view of ongoing operations and future possibilities in the Comstock Lode, the Green River coal basin, and the Colorado mines. At Comstock, Hague took careful note of everything from timbers and shafts to pumps, drills, and hoisting works—all illustrated with detailed drawings and O'Sullivan's remarkable underground photographs. With an eye to future investment, Hague reviewed the activities of the leading mining companies, reporting on current costs and possible profits. Turning his attention to the Green River region, Hague confidently predicted that "it can be said with perfect safety that the [Green River basin] contains a practically inexhaustible supply of coal."[14] But no place more fully seized Hague's imagination than Colorado. Gold, silver, and coal all seemed present there in abundance. Looking to Colorado's future, the geologist was sure that "an unprecedented advance in the development of its natural resources may be expected."[15]

For all its success, the King survey did not bode well for the future of army exploration in the West. Despite funds and supplies from the War Department, no one could miss the fact that King and his fellow explorers were civilians, not soldiers. King's lifelong friend Henry Adams went so far as to write that the survey was a civilian, not a military, undertaking. General Humphreys was justifiably proud of the army's role in the King survey, but even he could not deny what was increasingly plain. The expedition's energy and intellect came not from the army but from the halls of universities and civilian centers like the Smithsonian Institution. With Clarence King the days of the soldier-explorers were both numbered and running out.

Clarence King was surely a man who defined Mark Twain's Gilded Age. Equally passionate in search of personal fame, glamorous adventure, and objective scientific truth, King was like Twain's Colonel Sellers, a larger-than-life character "at the center of the manufacture of gigantic schemes, of speculations of all sorts, of political and social gossip."[16] If anything, George Montague Wheeler was a man born past his time. The last of the great soldier-explorers, Wheeler should have marched with Frémont or been part of one of the Pacific railroad survey expeditions. Instead, by the time he graduated from West Point in 1866, the newly minted second lieutenant seemed bound for one routine garrison assignment after another.

What saved Wheeler from that dreary future was his distinguished academic record at West Point and marriage into the politically powerful Blair family. Posted to California, Wheeler first practiced his skills as a military topographer under the guidance of Colonel Robert S. Williamson. In 1869 Wheeler led his first exploring expedition—a standard military reconnaissance of southern and eastern Nevada. That experience prompted him to formulate grander plans for a vast area survey of the West beyond the 100th meridian. Perhaps the eager lieutenant thought it was still possible to be a latter-day Frémont or Emory.

The ambitious plans of a young officer in a remote part of the West would have gone nowhere except for General Humphreys' larger concerns. Always ready to advance the army's exploration role, Humphreys worried about the growing influence of the western surveys led by Ferdinand Vandiveer Hayden and John Wesley Powell. These were civilian expeditions under the aegis of the Department of Interior. And while Humphreys was King's patron, the general could not overlook that fact that King and his principal investigators were civilians as well. If the army was to remain a player in the western exploration game, soldier-explorers had to get back on the field. And the War Department had tactical concerns as well. As the potential for conflict with Indian nations intensified during the early 1870s, it was plain that the department lacked detailed maps for the far Southwest. A survey of the sort proposed by Wheeler could reinvigorate army exploration and provide needed military information as well.

Clarence King wrote his own exploration instructions; George Wheeler did not have that luxury. In late March 1871 General Humphreys sent Wheeler a carefully prepared exploration plan. The geographic range of Wheeler's exploration was defined as "those portions of the United States territory lying south of the Central Pacific Railroad, embracing Eastern Nevada and Arizona."[17] Eventually Wheeler's survey extended over 359,065 square miles, in the present-day states of New Mexico, Arizona, Utah, California, Colorado, Wyoming, Nebraska, and Montana.

Having set the geographical range, Humphreys also established Wheeler's exploration priorities. Reflecting the long army tradition of topographical cartography, Wheeler was ordered to "prepare accurate maps" of the country he explored. "In making this the main object," Humphreys wrote, "it is at the same time intended that you ascertain as far as practicable everything relating to the physical features of the country, the numbers, habits, and dispositions of the Indians who may live in this section, [and] the selection of such sites as may be of use for future military operations or occupation."[18]

Like others at the time, Humphreys imagined a West occupied by American farmers and miners, a region fully integrated into the national economy. Railroads were essential for such a future, and Wheeler was directed to locate and describe "the facilities offered for making rail or common roads, to meet the wants of those who at some future period may occupy or traverse this part of our territory." By the time Humphreys sent Wheeler into the field most promoters of western economic development centered their attention on corporate-sized mining ventures or large-scale agriculture. Wheeler was directed to pay special attention to "the mineral resources that may be discovered" and whenever possible to make "minute and detailed examinations of the locality and character of the deposits."[19] Unwilling to abandon the promise of the West as a farmer's paradise, Humphreys also ordered Wheeler to evaluate climate and native plants with an eye toward future farming and grazing operations.

George M. Wheeler as a United States Military Academy cadet.

With what he imagined as a broad exploration mandate, Wheeler enlisted an impressive expedition corps. Lieutenants David A. Lyle and Daniel W. Lockwood came from the army, as did Acting Assistant Surgeon Walter J. Hoffman. Timothy O'Sullivan, already an experienced traveler with the King survey, joined William Bell as Wheeler's photographers. Perhaps the most important appointment came when Wheeler recruited Grove Karl Gilbert, a distinguished geologist destined to become one of the most influential scientists for the study of western landscapes. Like other western survey leaders in the 1870s, Wheeler understood the value of publicity. To keep his expedition in the news he brought along Frederick W. Loring, a Boston journalist. Wheeler was not the best trained scientist to lead a survey expedition but he was determined not to lose the public relations battle.

The Wheeler survey—now carrying the grand title "Geographic Surveys West of the 100th Meridian"—began almost a decade of field work in early May 1871. Heading into Nevada, Wheeler and his men made a harrowing journey across Death Valley. Neither the first to cross it nor to name it, the soldier-explorer did describe the trek in a short, vivid account. "The stifling heat, great radiation, and constant glare from the sand were almost overpowering, and two of the command succumbed near nightfall, rendering it necessary to pack one man on the back of a mule."[20] Having survived this ordeal,

Wheeler and his men pursued their second objective. For many years the army had been interested in the course of the Colorado River. As early as 1857 Lieutenant Joseph Christmas Ives had led a pioneering scientific survey as far up the river as Black Canyon. Despite the first Powell expedition (1869) and a second Powell venture in 1871-72, Wheeler was determined to make his own river passage. In the fall of 1871 the Wheeler expedition struggled up the Colorado in the journey that yielded significant hardship and insignificant scientific results.

Over the next eight years, until the survey was ended in June 1879, Wheeler's men tramped the West. In his final report Wheeler summed up all the difficulties connected with so vast and complex a survey. The soldier-explorer had tried to develop a system for surveying and classifying large areas and then producing "accurate topographical maps, useful in military operations and administration at a minimum cost."[21] His solution came in two parts: first, "a mathematically connected net-work of established points"; and second, a series of 94 survey quadrants for the entire West. Wheeler was convinced that if his exploration had not been terminated in 1879 he could have produced "the first general survey of this region within the limits affixed."[22]

The seven sparsely-illustrated volumes of Wheeler's *Geographical Surveys West of the 100th Meridian* appeared between 1877 and 1889. Writing about those reports, historian Donald Worster observed that they were "an extraordinary compendium of useful information."[23] Much of that useful information was about land and economic development. In his usual methodical way Wheeler fashioned a land classification scheme that included farmland (with or without irrigation), grazing ranges, forest resources, wetlands, and arid regions. Like many others, Wheeler was convinced that irrigation would be the West's great hope. As he explained in his final report, "the probable future agricultural population of the area surveyed will be governed as much, if not more by the permanent supply of water than by the acreage available."[24]

While the Wheeler volumes included some important information about native peoples and cultures—including reports by H. C. Yarrow, Oscar Loew, and Frederick W. Putnam— Wheeler, in Donald Worster's estimation, "understood his survey to be another instrument, along with cannons and cavalry, of military conquest."[25] Like many other white Americans, Wheeler was persuaded that "the fate of the Indian is sealed."[26] However, he also thought that the future held more violence between native peoples and white outsiders. In many ways Wheeler's fierce animosity against Indians was fuelled by a bloody incident in November 1871 when expedition journalist Frederick Loring was killed in an Indian attack on a stagecoach at Wickenburg, Arizona.

Memories of that incident were still fresh when Wheeler prepared his final report. In a remarkable passage the soldier-explorer summed up his entire vision of the western future and the fate of native peoples. "Reflection makes it apparent that not only is the large area reserved greatly in excess of any actual need of the Indians, especially when their roving and predatory habits are abandoned, but also that these large tracts impede the harmonious

"Grand Cañon of the Colorado River, Mouth of Kanab Wash (south view),"
by William Bell.

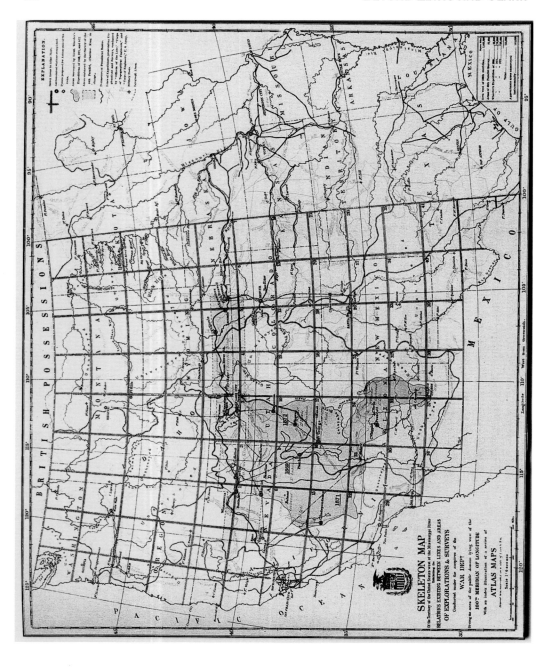

"Skeleton Map of the Territory of the United States west of the Mississippi River Exhibiting the Relations Existing between Lines and Areas of Explorations and Surveys Conducted under the Auspices of the War Dept.," by George M. Wheeler (1874).

and homogenous settlement of these regions, now being availed of for farms, homes, mines, mills, and workshops. The ever-restless surging tide of population, almost a law unto itself, already in many cases crowd over the borders of these reservations, and the time is not far distant when the question of the surrender of these lands to actual settlers will be naturally answered in the affirmative, on the plea of the greatest good for the greatest number."[27] Wheeler had gridded the lands, totaled up their value, mentally dispossessed native inhabitants, and envisioned an American West without Indians.

The story of what are sometimes called the Territorial Surveys usually centers on the expeditions led by King, Wheeler, Hayden, and Powell. But while the army invested most of it energies in the Southwest in the 1870s, there was at least one revealing exploration moment on the northern Great Plains—an episode of enduring consequence and national significance.

The name George Armstrong Custer is rarely associated with the Euro-American explorers of the American West. Custer seems so much a part of the Indian Wars that linking him to the journeys of soldier-explorers like Emory or Wheeler at first makes little sense. But in 1874—while Wheeler was in the field and King was busy preparing his elegant reports—Custer and the Seventh Cavalry made a reconnaissance-in-force into the Black Hills. It was an exploring venture that proved to have unforeseen consequences.

In many ways Custer's Black Hills expedition had its origins in the events and confusions spawned by the Fort Laramie Treaty of 1868. At the end of the Civil War, violence seemed everywhere on the northern plains. Plains Indians deeply resented the presence of army posts on the Bozeman Trail and the tidal wave of miners flooding into the Montana gold fields. The Fetterman Massacre (1866) increased tensions and, in the words of historian Francis Paul Prucha, "made clear in the East the seriousness of the Indian situation in the West."[28] In the spring of 1868 members of the United States Indian Peace Commission met with the northern plains tribes at Fort Laramie. Throughout that spring treaties were signed with the Brulé Sioux, the Crows, the Northern Cheyennes, and the Northern Arapahoes. Other Sioux bands gradually came in to "touch the pen" to the treaty paper. Because the Union Pacific Railroad had made steady westward progress, federal officials were willing to abandon the Bozeman Trail forts. From a Native American perspective the most important part of the treaty was Article Twelve. That provision established the Great Sioux Reservation, stretching from the Missouri River to the western boundary of Dakota Territory. Federal officials promised that there would be no further land cessions without the approval of three-fourths of male Indians either living on the reservation or having an "interest" in it. At a time when mineral rushes were transforming the western country from California and Nevada to Idaho and Montana, the 1868 treaty seemed to promise some security for northern plains Indians.

But that sense of security was soon tested by the power of illusion and the lure of gold. Well before the Civil War rumors drifted around that there was gold in what white Americans called the Black Hills, lands held sacred by the Lakota people. In the 1850s those rumors spread, urged on in part by rushes in California and Montana. By 1861 rumor hardened into belief when a group of Yankton promoters formed the Black Hills Exploring and Mining Association. Enthusiasm for the project waned during the war, but in 1865 the idea gained new life when the Legislative Assembly of Dakota Territory asked Congress to authorize a geological survey of the area under military auspices. But all those plans, schemes, and enthusiasms seemed to die when the 1868 treaty closed the Black Hills to miners.

Not everyone in Dakota Territory either supported or accepted the provisions of the Fort Laramie agreement. The lure of gold and the possibility of additional economic gains proved ever stronger. Newspapers like the Yankton *Press and Dakotaian* and the Sioux City *Times* criticized the treaty and urged that the Black Hills be "opened" to industrious American miners. But no one was more forceful in describing the full range of the region's profit-making possibilities than Judge W. W. Brookings of Yankton. "There are other sources of wealth in the Black Hills beside gold. We want the lumber to build our cities and towns, and the fact that there is an abundance of pine there will be an additional inducement to stimulate the enterprise."[29] The initial federal response to all this talk was sharp and quick. Secretary of the Interior Columbus Delano demanded that territorial governor John Burbank "put a stop" to any moves into lands guaranteed by the Fort Laramie Treaty. The War Department made its feelings known as well. General Alfred Terry, commanding the Department of Dakota, wrote a stern letter to newspaper editor Charles Collins reminding him that anyone entering the Black Hills would be restrained by military force if necessary.

But dreams die hard and in 1874 the possibility of Black Hills gold in white hands found fresh life in a surprising source. The War Department had steadfastly opposed any white presence in the region. But by 1874 the northern plains military situation seemed to have changed. After an inspection tour in the spring of the year, General Philip H. Sheridan—commander of the Division of Missouri—was persuaded that the only way to stop Indian raiders from moving easily out of Dakota Territory into Nebraska was to establish a post in the Black Hills area. In order to do that, the army needed to mount an exploring expedition to reconnoiter and map the region.

In early May 1874 plans were being made for companies of the Seventh Cavalry to undertake such a journey. This was not the first time that Custer and his troopers had been part of an exploring venture. In the summer of 1873 Custer's command participated in a major military-scientific reconnaissance into present-day Montana. With that experience behind him, Custer began to plan a large-scale expedition. Black Hills promoters were now convinced that federal policy had changed. The gold was there, Custer would find it, and Dakota Territory would become another California.

As Custer assembled and outfitted his military force, he also acquired what might be termed his scientific corps. On the Montana expedition in the previous year General Sheridan had ordered that "all officers and persons on the expedition are charged...to aid in the collection and preservation of knowledge."[30] Custer surely had no professional interest in scientific exploration, and his Black Hills adventure was not at first intended as a scientific enterprise. But that changed when Sheridan invited his friend, the distinguished Yale pale-ontologist, Othniel C. Marsh, to join the journey. Marsh politely said no but sent his young, ambitious assistant, George Bird Grinnell.

In late May, as the pace of preparations quickened, Custer requested a geologist. Per-haps with gold on his mind, he asked: "Is there no way by which the service of a geologist can be had with the expedition? The country to be visited is so new and believed to be so interesting that it will be a pity not to improve to the fullest extent the opportunity to determine all that is possible of its character, scientific and otherwise."[31] When General Humphreys indicated that his current budget did not allow funds to hire a geologist, the state of Minnesota provided Newton H. Winchell as well as botanist A. B. Donaldson. At the beginning of the new fiscal year federal monies were provided for Winchell.

To round out the civilian scientific corps, William H. Illingworth joined as expedition photographer. By 1874 photography had become an established part of western explora-tion, thanks to the pioneering efforts of John Mix Stanley, Timothy O'Sullivan, William Bell, and Jack Hillers. Illingworth got his first western experience in 1867 as part of an exploring party into Montana Territory. Recruited by Corps of Engineers Captain William Ludlow, the St. Paul-based photographer proved a disappointment. More interested in making stereoscope views for sale than providing a scientific record, Illingworth finally found himself in court charged by Ludlow with embezzling federal property.

With his attention mostly fixed on the Wheeler and King surveys, and knowing that Congress was about to launch a probe into the entire western survey question, General Humphreys could hardly be expected to pay much attention to a short foray into the Black Hills. But the Custer expedition was an army operation, and Humphreys' man on that journey was Captain William Ludlow. West Point Class of 1864 and an experienced field engineer, Ludlow had surveyed the Yellowstone River as part of the Montana expedition of 1873 and understood the problems he would face in making observations during a rapid march. Six enlisted men and civilian topographer W. H. Wood assisted Ludlow.

No Custer outfit ever went into the field without an adequate supply of journalists. Custer was news, the Seventh's commanding officer wanted to make news, and gold in the Black Hills was bound to be news. William E. Curtis wrote for the Chicago *Inter-Ocean* and was a stringer for the New York *World*. Nathan H. Knappen represented Bismarck's *Tribune*. Samuel J. Burrows had reported on the 1873 Montana venture and was now ready to tell readers of New York's *Tribune* all about the army's latest western adventure.

The Black Hills expedition left Fort Abraham Lincoln on July 2 with ten companies of the Seventh Cavalry, two infantry companies, and 110 wagons and ambulances. For the next two months the expedition snaked its way into the heart of the Black Hills. At the beginning of the journey many believed that there were large numbers of Indians in the region. Yet the expedition encountered few, giving rise to the notion that miners coming to

*Photograph taken by William Illingsworth during George Armstrong
Custer's Black Hills expedition in 1874.*

the elusive gold deposits would meet no native resistance. And no one doubted that the miners would come. In fact, there were two miners—Horatio N. Ross and William McKay—who simply attached themselves to the expedition. When Ross and McKay found what they claimed was gold in today's Custer Park on French Creek in late July, the stage was set for unimagined trouble.

On July 27 Captain Ludlow noted in his official journal that "the gold-hunters were very busy all day with shovel and pan exploring the streams."[32] Over the next few days the miners "redoubled their efforts."[33] Finally, on August 2, with the entire expedition buzzing about gold, Ludlow went to Custer's tent and saw "what the miner said he obtained during the day." Unimpressed by what seemed tiny pin heads of an unidentified mineral, Ludlow cautiously noted that the miners "expressed themselves quite confident that if they should reach bedrock in the valleys at a favorable place, plenty could be obtained by use of the pan."[34]

Custer himself was persuaded that "veins of what the geologists term gold-bearing quartz crop out on almost every hillside."[35] Determined to get the news out, on August 3 Custer ordered scout Charley Reynolds to make a dashing ride to Fort Laramie. From there

Reynolds reached Sioux City, Iowa, on August 13. By now the news was everywhere, and even though Reynolds said he never saw any gold and Captain Ludlow doubted its very existence, the Black Hills gold rush was on. The very day Reynolds reached Sioux City, the Yankton *Press and Dakotaian* boldly reported that "Rich mines of Gold and Silver Reported Found by Custer." Recalling the Panic of 1873 that wreaked havoc on the national economy, the newspaper claimed: "The National Debt to be Paid when Custer Returns."[36] El Dorado was found at last in the Black Hills.

Despite the fact that both Captain Ludlow and geologist Newton Winchell rejected such claims as nonsense, gold fever gripped the region. The first group of gold seekers left Sioux City in October and were turned back by military units enforcing the 1868 treaty. At first the army did its best to keep gold hunters out of the hills. But when negotiations begun by President Grant aimed at convincing the Sioux to relocate to Indian Territory failed, the president quietly withdrew military patrols in November 1874. By the spring of 1875, adventurers were coming in ever-increasing numbers. The Indian response was prompt as individual miners were killed. Those deaths, and the growing tensions in the Black Hills, set the stage for the Centennial Campaign of 1876 and the Battle of Little Bighorn. The line is not a simple, direct one from the Black Hills in 1874 to the Greasy Grass in 1876. Custer's exploration of the Black Hills, like all Euro-American exploration, was driven by a complex set of passions, illusions, and ambitions. The road into and out of the Black Hills had stops along the way in New York banking houses, Washington, D.C., government departments, and newspaper offices in Yankton and Sioux City.

By the mid 1870s the federal government was funding western surveys conducted by King, Wheeler, Hayden, and Powell. In addition there were smaller-scale army ventures like Custer's Black Hills reconnaissance. During the summer of 1874 there was the embarrassing scene of Wheeler surveyors bumping up against those from the Hayden expedition, all training their instruments on the same western landscape. A Congress made budget-conscious by the economic upheavals of 1873 was persuaded that this was the time to investigate the whole western survey situation. General Humphreys initiated and welcomed the hearings, convinced that the army had the best record for scientific exploration. The chief engineer was persuaded that the Townsend Committee on Public Lands would eventually cut the Interior Department out of the exploration business and consolidate all surveys in the War Department.

But Humphreys did not reckon with the political skill of Ferdinand V. Hayden and his ally, James T. Gardner. Hayden had long been critical of the soldier-explorers and Gardner—who had once worked so effectively for King—had left King for Hayden. Together they wielded considerable influence both in Congress and in academic circles. The hearings did not go well for the army. Hayden and Gardner succeeded in portraying soldier-explorers as old-fashioned, fussy naturalists while civilian surveys represented the best of modern science. In a grumpy mood, Wheeler refused to testify. The hearings were punctuated by dramatic moments, as when congressmen heard testimony that Hayden had threatened to "utterly crush" Wheeler.[37]

Thanks to support from President Grant, army exploration survived, but it was a near miss. The Townsend Committee reported that "each of the survey parties has been doing very excellent work for the benefit of the people and appropriate for the particular end it had in view." Social Darwinism—the ruling business ideology of the day—heaped praise on competitive robber barons. Perhaps scientists could advance the empire of the mind by the same iron laws of the marketplace. But the committee did recognize that "the time is approaching, however, when it may be proper to consolidate them."[38]

Even so steadfast a defender of the soldier-explorers as General Humphreys must have recognized that a era was slipping away. In 1878 the House Committee on Appropriations halted all further survey funding, pending a nonpartisan investigation. With Grant out of office and the army increasingly unpopular with humanitarian reformers, the game was almost done. John Wesley Powell seemed to catch the mood of the moment when he wrote that "the present multiplication of organizations is unscientific, excessively expensive, and altogether vicious, preventing comprehensive, thorough, and honest research, stimulating unhealthy rivalry, and leading to the production of sensational and briefly popular rather than solid and enduring results."[39] A special committee of the National Academy of Sciences was charged with investigating the entire exploration mess and making recommendations. Chaired by Othniel Marsh and having no army representation, the committee generally discounted the contributions of the soldier-explorers and recommended consolidation of all the western expeditions under civilian control within the Department of the Interior. In 1879, with Wheeler still in the field, all surveys were combined into the United States Geological Survey under the leadership of Clarence King. What had begun in 1803 when Thomas Jefferson asked Captain Meriwether Lewis to organize a "tour" to the Pacific was now over.

Chapter *10*

FILLING UP THE CANVAS

*I*n late May 1805—at the very moment the Lewis and Clark expedition was working its way upriver to the Great Falls of the Missouri—Thomas Jefferson offered his friend William Dunbar the following prophecy. "We shall delineate with correctness the great arteries of this great country: those who come after us will extend the ramifications as they become acquainted with them, and fill up the canvas we begin."[1] The president offered a powerful set of images, suggesting both an American future and the role of the army in fashioning that future. The continent was laced with rivers—highways of commerce and empire. American explorers would trace those rivers to their sources and build an empire. Then, shifting the metaphor, the entire continent became an artist's canvas. Rivers were the outlines in a drawing and explorers would fill in the blank spaces, making empire a work of art. Never mind that Jefferson's supposedly blank canvas was the product of erasure, the sweeping away of native North America. For the next seventy years soldier-explorers followed the rivers, marked the trails, and filled in the outlines by way of maps, journals, drawings, photographs, and objects of every sort.

George M. Wheeler, the last in a long line of soldier-explorers, sensed that the tradition of military exploration in the West was coming to an end in the late 1870s. Writing to General Humphreys, Wheeler dramatically pronounced that "the day of the pathfinder has sensibly ended."[2] While Wheeler hoped that army exploration might continue with a more modern, scientific approach, his line had an obituary air about it. For all sorts of reasons—institutional, cultural, and personal—the age of Lewis and Clark, Frémont, and Emory had passed. In countless journeys often made under the most difficult conditions, soldier-explorers mapped the continent and defined the American empire. There was nothing romantic or glorious about that work. William H. Emory once described it as "dreary and thankless." It was the tedious labor in making and recording thousands of latitude and longitude calculations, and an endless number of triangulations and altitude measurements. There were days bent over a drafting table or squinting through a sextant. And there were endless hours spent in writing, photographing, and collecting—to say nothing of wrestling with bulky equipment, balky mules, and unpredictable weather. Behind Meriwether Lewis's "seens of visionary inchantment" were all the physical, emotional, and intellectual challenges of constant travel in demanding, often unforgiving country.

Now, more than a century after the soldier-explorers slipped into the western past, it seems plain that all those journeys left behind a complex inheritance, one that links our past to our present. Army explorers were agents of empire. They were the vanguard in a burst of geographic expansion with continental sweep and global consequence. From the Ohio Indian Wars of the 1780s to the Wounded Knee Massacre in 1890, the army was at the point of the American thrust into the West. Military explorers mapped the country and scouted those who resisted or stood in the way of the American invasion. As the military arm of the United States, the army did the nation's bidding and never more enthusiastically than in the West. While a few regular officers expressed doubts about territorial expansion, soldier-explorers generally embraced Manifest Destiny and were often its most forceful proponents. To separate explorers like William Clark, John C. Frémont, and William H. Emory from the larger story of western invasion and conquest is to tell only half the story and from one side of the cultural and political divide. Opening the West for some meant closing it for others.

But to brand the soldier-explorers as simply the advance guard for what George M. Wheeler called "the ever restless surging tide of population" makes for all too simple a story. The journeys of the army explorers marked the foundations of a western empire. Those same journeys expanded the empire of the mind as well. The official War Department obituary for Colonel Abert, issued on January 29, 1863, suggests a second, enduring legacy of the soldier-explorers. "The geographical and other information concerning this continent which its [the Corps of Topographical Engineers] officers have collected and published, has challenged the admiration of the scientific world; while the practical benefit of their labors has been felt in nearly every State and every Territory; the whole forming a proud monument to him who was its founder."[3] That "proud monument" was built on scores of published exploration narratives, important descriptions of geological formations and terrain features, landmark maps, memorable drawings, paintings, and photographs, comprehensive enthnographic studies, and specimens that enriched museums and laboratories. Soldier-explorers enlarged the boundaries of the American mind, making the West part of the nation's intellectual as well as geographic domain. Trails and tracks, voyages of discovery, and journeys of empire shaped the history of the American West. The soldier-explorers followed those trails and marked those tracks. If so many of their names are lost to us today, it is because their journeys have gone deep into the fabric of American life. Wheeler once talked about the "great and special wonders" of the West.[4] The soldier-explorers represented a nation determined to claim those wonders for its own. Filling in Jefferson's canvas, the soldier-explorers made the West part of the nation.

Suggested Readings

*A*ny march with the soldier-explorers must begin with William H. Goetzmann's *Army Exploration in the American West, 1803-1863* (New Haven: Yale University Press, 1959). Goetzmann continues the army story in *Exploration and Empire: The Explorer and the Scientist in the Winning of the American West* (New York: Random House, 1966). Also of enduring value are: Richard A. Bartlett, *Great Surveys of the American West* (Norman: University of Oklahoma Press, 1962) and Herman J. Viola, *Exploring the West* (Washington, D.C.: Smithsonian Books, 1987).

Useful for placing the soldier-explorers in the larger military context is Michael L. Tate, *The Frontier Army in the Settlement of the West* (Norman: University of Oklahoma Press, 1999). That military context is fully treated in two seminal books by Robert M. Utley: *Frontiersmen in Blue: The United States Army and the Indian, 1848-1865* (New York: Macmillan Company, 1967) and *Frontier Regulars: The United States Army and the Indian, 1866-1890* (New York: Macmillan Company, 1973). The exploration story is also told in three essays: James P. Ronda, "Exploring the West in the Age of Jefferson"; Vincent Ponko, Jr., "The Military Explorers of the American West, 1838-1860"; and Richard A. Bartlett, "Scientific Exploration of the American West, 1865-1900"—all printed in John L. Allen, ed., *North American Exploration: A Continent Comprehended*, vol. 3 (Lincoln: University of Nebraska Press, 1997).

The Lewis and Clark expedition has generated a literature large in size and varied in quality. The best introduction remains Donald Jackson, *Thomas Jefferson and the Stony Mountains: Exploring the West from Monticello* (Urbana: University of Illinois Press, 1981), recently retitled in the University of Oklahoma Press reprint as *Thomas Jefferson and the Rocky Mountains*. Also useful are John L. Allen, *Passage through the Garden: Lewis and Clark and the Image of the American Northwest* (Urbana: University of Illinois Press, 1973) and James P. Ronda, *Lewis and Clark among the Indians* (Lincoln: University of Nebraska Press, 1984).

Zebulon Montgomery Pike still waits for a modern biographer. The best short introduction is in Jackson, *Thomas Jefferson and the Stony Mountains* and in Jackson's edition of the Pike letters and journals. The Stephen H. Long expedition is ably discussed in

Roger L. Nichols and Patrick L. Halley, *Stephen Long and American Frontier Exploration* (Reprint, Norman: University of Oklahoma Press, 1995). George J. Goodman and Cheryl A. Lawson, *Retracing Major Stephen H. Long's 1820 Expedition: The Itinerary and Botany* (Norman: University of Oklahoma Press, 1995) is a model for superb scholarship and exhaustive scientific fieldwork.

The related subjects of Manifest Destiny and the Mexican War have prompted a large and often controversial body of writing. The classic account remains Albert K. Weinberg, *Manifest Destiny: A Study of Nationalist Expansionism in American History* (Baltimore: Johns Hopkins University Press, 1935). Anders Stephanson, *Manifest Destiny: American Expansionism and the Empire of Right* (New York: Hill and Wang, 1995) is a more modern account. Thomas R. Hietala, *Manifest Design: Anxious Aggrandizement in Late Jacksonian America* (Ithaca: Cornell University Press, 1985) is filled with important insights about the period. Also useful for its focus on army officers is Samuel J. Watson, "The Uncertain Road to Manifest Destiny: Army Officers and the Course of American Territorial Expansionism," in Sam W. Haynes and Christopher Morris, eds., *Manifest Destiny and Empire: American Antebellum Expansionism* (College Station: Texas A & M University Press, 1997). The larger issues raised by the Mexican War are ably discussed in Robert W. Johannsen, *To the Halls of the Montezumas: The Mexican War in the American Imagination* (New York: Oxford University Press, 1985). The military context in which soldier-explorers like William H. Emory worked is treated in James M. McCaffrey, *Army of Manifest Destiny: The American Soldier in the Mexican War, 1846-1848* (New York: New York University Press, 1992).

Biography remains one of the most popular ways to study the soldier-explorers. John Charles Frémont has attracted a number of biographers, including Allan Nevins (1939), Ferol Egan (1977), and Andrew Rolle (1991). Tom Chaffin's *Pathfinder: John Charles Frémont and the Course of American Empire* (New York: Hill and Wang, 2002) is the best recent biography. Kent D. Richards, *Isaac I. Stevens: Young Man in a Hurry* (Pullman: Washington State University Press, 1979) remains the standard treatment of that ambitious soldier-explorer. William H. Emory's long and important career as a soldier-explorer is discussed in L. David Norris, James C. Milligan, and Odie B. Faulk, *William H. Emory: Soldier-Scientist* (Tucson: University of Arizona Press, 1998).

The classic biography of Clarence King is by Thurman Wilkins, first published in 1953 and reprinted by the University of New Mexico Press in 1988. King remains such a compelling figure that he deserves another look. Stephen J. Pyne, *Grove Karl Gilbert: A Great Engine of Research* (Austin: University of Texas Press, 1980) centers on a remarkable figure in the history of western exploration and American science. While John Wesley Powell was not a soldier-explorer, his life and travels illuminate what the army was all about in the West. The best recent biography is Donald Worster, *A River Running West: The Life of John Wesley Powell* (New York: Oxford University Press, 2001).

An appreciation for cartography and the role of photography is essential to a broader understanding of the soldier-explorers. The standard work on western cartography remains

Carl I. Wheat, *Mapping the Trans-Mississippi West, 1540-1861*, 5 vols. (Menlo Park, California: Institute for Historical Cartography, 1958-1962). Exploration photography is treated with great sensitivity in Martha A. Sandweiss, *Print the Legend: Photography and the American West* (New Haven: Yale University Press, 2002).

The distinguished documentary editor Donald Jackson once wrote that Lewis and Clark were the "writingest" explorers in American history. Much the same can be said for many of the other soldier-explorers. Their reports take modern readers into the very heart of the West. There is no better way to understand the soldier-explorers and the complex times in which they lived than to read what they wrote. Their words—sometimes troubling and always challenging—are foundation texts for a deeper history of the American West.

Notes

CHAPTER 1. LEWIS AND CLARK—CAPTAINS WEST

1. Jefferson to Adams, Monticello, 10 June 1815, Lester J. Cappon, ed., *The Adams-Jefferson Letters*, 2 vols. (Chapel Hill: University of North Carolina Press, 1959), 2:443.

2. W. Kaye Lamb, ed., *The Journals and Letters of Sir Alexander Mackenzie* (Cambridge, England: The Hakluyt Society, 1970), 417.

3. Donald Jackson, ed., *The Letters of the Lewis and Clark Expedition with Related Documents, 1783-1854*, second ed., 2 vols. (Urbana: University of Illinois Press, 1978), 2:654.

4. Lincoln to Jefferson, Washington, D.C., 17 April 1803, *ibid.*, 1:35.

5. Jefferson to Lewis, Washington, D.C., 20 June 1803, *ibid.*, 1:61.

6. John L. Allen, *Passage through the Garden: Lewis and Clark and the Image of the American Northwest* (Urbana: University of Illinois Press, 1975), 23.

7. Gary E. Moulton, ed., *The Journals of the Lewis and Clark Expedition*, 13 vols. (Lincoln: University of Nebraska Press, 1983-2001), 2:215.

8. Jefferson to Lewis, Washington, D.C., 20 June 1803, Jackson, ed., *Letters of the Lewis and Clark Expedition*, 1:62.

9. *JLCE*, 6:49.

10. *JLCE*, 6:48.

11. *JLCE*, 10:171.

12. *JLCE*, 6:53.

13. Jefferson to William Dunbar, Washington, D.C., 25 May 1805, Jackson, ed., *Letters of the Lewis and Clark Expedition*, 1:245.

CHAPTER 2. THE ADVENTURES OF ZEBULON MONTGOMERY PIKE

1. The line comes from Donald Jackson, who repeated it often in conversation with the author.

2. Wilkinson to Dearborn, St. Louis, 26 November 1805, Donald Jackson, ed., *The Journals of Zebulon Montgomery Pike with Letters and Related Documents*, 2 vols. (Norman: University of Oklahoma Press, 1966), 2:250.

3. Pike to David Bissell, St. Louis, 15 June 1806, *ibid.*, 2:114.

4. Wilkinson to Pike, St. Louis, 25 June 1806, *ibid.*, 2:285-86.

5. Pike to Wilkinson, LaCharette, 22 July 1806, *ibid.*, 2:124.

6. Jackson, ed., *Journals of Zebulon Montgomery Pike*, 1:358.

7. *Ibid.*, 1:367.